Judges

INTERPRETATION
A Bible Commentary for Teaching and Preaching

INTERPRETATION
A BIBLE COMMENTARY FOR TEACHING AND PREACHING

James Luther Mays, *Editor*
Patrick D. Miller, *Old Testament Editor*
Paul J. Achtemeier, *New Testament Editor*

J. CLINTON McCANN

Judges

INTERPRETATION

A Bible Commentary
for Teaching and Preaching

John Knox Press
LOUISVILLE

For Lucy Webb Malone,
whose faithful study of and living of the Word
has been and will remain an inspiration
to me and to many.

Library of Congress Cataloging-in-Publication Data

McCann, J. Clinton, 1951–
 Judges / J. Clinton McCann.— 1st ed.
  p. cm. — (Interpretation, a Bible commentary for teaching and preaching)
 Includes bibliographical references.
 ISBN 0-8042-3107-9 (alk. paper)
 1. Bible. O.T. Judges—Commentaries. I. Title. II. Series.

 BS1305.53 .M33 2002
 222'.3207—dc21   2002072450

© copyright J. Clinton McCann 2002
This book is printed on acid-free paper that meets the American National Standards Institute Z39.48 standard. ⊗
02 03 04 05 06 07 08 09 10 11 — 10 9 8 7 6 5 4 3 2 1
Printed in the United States of America
John Knox Press
Louisville, Kentucky

SERIES PREFACE

This series of commentaries offers an interpretation of the books of the Bible. It is designed to meet the need of students, teachers, ministers, and priests for a contemporary expository commentary. These volumes will not replace the historical critical commentary or homiletical aids to preaching. The purpose of this series is rather to provide a third kind of resource, a commentary that presents the integrated result of historical and theological work with the biblical text.

An interpretation in the full sense of the term involves a text, an interpreter, and someone for whom the interpretation is made. Here, the text is what stands written in the Bible in its full identity as literature from the time of "the prophets and apostles," the literature that is read to inform, inspire, and guide the life of faith. The interpreters are scholars who seek to create an interpretation that is both faithful to the text and useful to the church. The series is written for those who teach, preach, and study the Bible in the community of faith.

The commentary generally takes the form of expository essays. It is planned and written in the light of the needs and questions that arise in the use of the Bible as Holy Scripture. The insights and results of contemporary scholarly research are used for the sake of the exposition. The commentators write as exegetes and theologians. The task that they undertake is both to deal with what the texts say and to discern their meaning for faith and life. The exposition is the unified work of one interpreter.

The text on which the comment is based is the Revised Standard Version of the Bible and, since its appearance, the New Revised Standard Version. The general availability of these translations makes the printing of a text in the commentary unnecessary. The commentators have also had other current versions in view as they worked and refer to their readings where it is helpful. The text is divided into sections appropriate to the particular book; comment deals with passages as a whole, rather than proceeding word by word, or verse by verse.

Writers have planned their volumes in light of the requirements set by the exposition of the book assigned to them. Biblical books differ in character, content, and arrangement. They also differ in the way they have been and are used in the liturgy, thought, and devotion of the church. The distinctiveness and use of particular books have been taken into account in decisions about the approach, emphasis, and use of space in the commentaries. The goal has been to allow writers to develop the format that provides for the best presentation of their interpretation.

The result, writers and editors hope, is a commentary that both explains and applies, an interpretation that deals with both the meaning and the significance of biblical texts. Each commentary reflects, of course, the writer's own approach and perception of the church and world. It could and should not be otherwise. Every interpretation of any kind is individual in that sense; it is one reading of the text. But all who work at the interpretation of the Scripture in the church need the help and stimulation of a colleague's reading and understanding of the text. If these volumes serve and encourage interpretation in that way, their preparation and publication will realize their purpose.

The Editors

AUTHOR'S PREFACE

Although largely ignored by the contemporary church, the book of Judges and its call to covenant loyalty are of paramount importance, especially in an era when so many things attempt to claim the attention and allegiance of the people of God. That the book of Judges has received so much scholarly attention in recent years is perhaps a good sign that it is on its way to being rediscovered. In any case, it is a pleasure and privilege to have joined the community of interpreters of the book of Judges and to have contributed, by way of this volume, to the ongoing discussion of the book of Judges and its significance for the contemporary church and world.

As always, the writing of a commentary is a communal endeavor, and I have learned from many persons. Some of them are mentioned by name in the commentary and bibliography, but there are many more persons to whom I am grateful. Thanks are due especially to Patrick D. Miller and James L. Mays, the series editors, who extended the invitation to write this volume and whose suggestions and guidance have helped immensely. I appreciate too the support of the community of teachers and learners at Eden Theological Seminary, including the Board of Directors (and their generous sabbatical policy), the administrative staff, my faculty colleagues, and the students, several of whom helped in a special way by participating in a master of divinity course on the book of Judges in the summer of 1998. I also taught adult education courses on the book of Judges at First Presbyterian Church, Kirkwood, Missouri, and Trinity Presbyterian Church, Little Rock, Arkansas; the questions, comments, and suggestions of the participants were very valuable.

Special thanks are due also to the persons who had a more direct hand in the process of the production of this volume. Sarah Fredriksen McCann, Victor H. Matthews, and Barbara and Mike Willock read the initial draft of the manuscript and offered insightful and helpful comments and advice. Victor, who is professor of religious studies at Southwest Missouri State University, was wonderfully generous with his time and his knowledge. Our conversations about the book of Judges were encouraging as well as educational. His sharing of bibliographical resources and written materials was of tremendous assistance to me, and I am very grateful.

Thanks too to Mary Swehla, administrative assistant to the Eden faculty. As always, she faithfully and efficiently word-processed the often barely legible manuscript that I produced with pen and paper.

As always too, my wife, Sarah Fredriksen McCann, and daughters, Jennifer Grace McCann and Sarah Carter McCann, have been constant sources of joy, encouragement, and support, as have the other members of my larger family. To one of them, Lucy Webb Malone, my ninety-one-year old great-aunt, this book is dedicated, in honor of her long and fruitful years of dedication to the study of Scripture and to the living of the Word with faithful simplicity, as a member of Trinity United Methodist Church in Petersburg, Virginia.

CONTENTS

INTERPRETATION

Introduction

1. Why Study the Book of Judges?

The book of Judges has a bad reputation. In fact, it seems to be the worst of what many people consider to be several rather bad Old Testament books. Along with the book of Joshua, perhaps, it is the book that people seem to have in mind when they say things like, "Let's not study the Old Testament. It's so full of violence and war and killing." Or, "I just don't like the Old Testament. God is so wrathful and vengeful. I like the New Testament, where God is love." Or, "How could God tell the Israelites to kill the Canaanites and all those other people? Jesus told us to love our enemies, not to kill them." And so on. The reputation of the book of Judges is apparently no better among the framers of the Revised Common Lectionary than it is among persons in the pew. In the three-year lectionary cycle of Old Testament lessons, the book of Judges is represented *one* time (Judges 4:1–7, Proper 28 [33], Year A).

Given its bad reputation, one might legitimately ask why we should even consider reading and studying the book of Judges. Why should we study it, write about it, teach about it, and preach from it? Don't we have enough violence nowadays on television and at the movies? Why do we need more of it at church? Isn't it bad enough that all that horrible stuff is in the Bible to start with? Do we have to make it worse by paying attention to it? Wouldn't the best policy be to just ignore it? The answer to this last question, in most ecclesiastical circles, seems to be *yes*. In short, the book of Judges seems to be an embarrassment to most church folk, and perhaps it is best passed over in silence. Hence it is necessary from the outset to make a case for teaching and preaching the book of Judges.

Given the situation just described, it may seem like special pleading to propose that the book of Judges may be the most timely and relevant of all the books in the Old Testament. Before dismissing this proposal as a poorly disguised attempt to justify the effort devoted to the writing of this volume, consider the following list of items:

- tension and strife between rival groups (in the Middle East or elsewhere)
- disputes over land and territory

1

- uncertainty over the roles of men and women
- power-hungry political leaders
- child abuse
- spouse abuse
- senseless and excessive violence
- male political leaders who chase women
- excessive individualism
- moral confusion
- social chaos

What time and place is being described by this list? It sounds as if the list could be characterizing the state of the world, especially the situation in the United States of America, in the early twenty-first century. But, in fact, the list is an accurate description of the contents of the book of Judges. The very first verse of the book introduces the strife between the Israelites and the Canaanites; and other groups will later enter the picture—the Midianites (chaps. 6—8), the Ammonites (chap. 11), the Philistines (chaps. 13—16). The disputes are over the control of land, which, in biblical terms, represents access to life. The story of Deborah, Barak, and Jael highlights the leadership of the two females, while Barak's role is minimal (chaps. 4–5); and several women are major characters throughout the book of Judges (see below, section 3d). While Gideon is generally viewed as a hero, he actually seems to center a great deal of power in himself (see 8:22–28), and his son Abimelech is a tyrant (chap. 9). Jephthah kills his daughter (chap. 11), and later a Levite abuses his wife both while she is alive and after she is killed (chap. 19). Samson has a seemingly uncontrollable desire for Philistine women (chaps. 13—16). His story is characterized by excessive violence, which only gets worse in chaps. 17—21, where, in the absence of a king, all the people are out for themselves (see 17:6; 18:1; 19:1; 21:25). The result is moral confusion and social chaos.

Unfortunately, all these realities sound strikingly familiar. While the world has obviously changed dramatically in the past three thousand years or so, and while human civilization has come a long way, the book of Judges is a timely reminder of how far we have *not* come. While we are inclined to think about all of the above issues and problems primarily in psychological, sociological, anthropological, or political terms, the book of Judges is an invitation to think also about ourselves and our world in *theological* terms. From the outset, the book of Judges urges us to confront the challenging claim that nothing will be right with our individual selves, our churches, or our world unless we, the people of God, manifest steadfast loyalty to God alone—in short, unless we are

2

faithful to the covenant between God and ourselves (see commentary on 1:1—2:5; 2:6—3:6).

But if the book of Judges offers a challenge, it is one that lies at the heart of the gospel. The gospel promises life, but the gift must be accepted and embraced. When it is not—that is, when we worship and serve something other than God—the results are destructive and ultimately deadly. The book of Judges documents Israel's discovery of this truth. The painful lesson that Israel learned can serve to instruct us as well. In short, the book of Judges is a warning, but the warning is grounded in hope; for, as the book of Judges relates, not only did Israel experience the destructive results of its own disloyalty and disobedience, but it also experienced a God who is unfailingly faithful to a faithless people. In a word, Israel experienced a God who is *gracious* (see below, section 4). These two simultaneous realities—warning and hope, judgment and grace—beg to be studied, taught, and proclaimed, as much in the contemporary church and world as they were in ancient Israel. (On preaching from the book of Judges, see Joseph R. Jeter Jr., *Preaching Judges*.)

2. The Judges: The Characters, the Period(s), and the Book

2a. What Were the Judges?

It is frequently pointed out that the word "judges" is a poor name for the book of Judges and an inaccurate description of its major characters. The term "judges" (Hebrew root *špt*) suggests to most people some sort of legal functionary—a black-robed person sitting behind a bench, holding a gavel, and making decisions on points of law. With the apparent exception of Deborah, who held court under the palm tree known by her name (Judg. 4:5), the judges do not seem to have been legal interpreters. (See also, however, 1 Sam. 7:15–17, where Samuel provides another apparent exception, although beyond the confines of the book of Judges.)

Indeed, it can be argued that the primary activity of the judges was leading the Israelites (or at least some of the Israelite tribes) against their oppressive enemies. Early in the book, individual judges are also called "deliverer" (3:9, 15; Hebrew *yš*ʻ); and the verb *yš*ʻ is often used to describe a judge's work (see 2:16; 3:31; 6:15; 8:22; 10:1; 13:5). Since the work of a "judge" or "deliverer" was apparently not completed immediately after a deliverance had been effected (see 2:18–19; 10:2–3), some scholars suggest that the term "judge" be understood in the broader sense of "ruler" or "governor." The Hebrew root *špt* can have this broader sense (see 1 Kgs. 3:9, where the two occurrences of *špt* are translated as "govern"), and this is a reasonable proposal.

3

Because the tradition is long-standing, this volume will ordinarily refer to the main characters of the book of Judges as "judges"; however, it should be noted from the outset that the root *špṭ* means not only "to judge" in the narrow sense, and not only "to govern" in the broader sense, but it also means in the broadest sense "to establish justice." For this reason, Jon L. Berquist has suggested that the Hebrew word normally translated "judge" be rendered instead as "bringer of justice" (Berquist, 91). This designation suggests that the judges were persons entrusted with the enactment of God's will for the world; this encompassed deliverance from external oppression (2:16, 18), leadership exercised to ensure the exclusive worship and service of God (2:19), and hence the creation of internal conditions that support life as God wills it to be.

That the judges should be understood in this comprehensive sense as establishers of justice is suggested by the current form and placement of the book of Judges. The judges are portrayed, in some sense at least, as successors of Joshua (see 1:1 and 2:6–23, noting that "Joshua" appears in both v. 6 and v. 23). Joshua in turn is portrayed as the successor of Moses (see Josh. 1:1). Moses received the torah, according to the books of Exodus through Deuteronomy; Joshua is to be the guardian of the torah (Josh. 1:8–9). The intent of the torah is to ensure the exclusive worship of God (see Exod. 20:1–7) and the establishment of conditions that sustain human life as God intends it (see Exod. 20:8–17). Fundamental for life as God intends it, according to the torah, are "justice" and "righteousness" (see Deut. 16:18–19; "justice" in v. 18 is Hebrew *mišpaṭ*, while the two occurrences of "justice" in v. 19 are Hebrew *ṣedeq*, a virtual synonym, usually translated "righteousness," that often is paired with the root *špṭ* or occurs in conjunction with it, as in Pss. 72:1; 96:13; 98:9; Amos 5:24). Thus, as successors to Moses and Joshua, the judges are to be, in the most comprehensive sense, mediators of the covenant, at the heart of which was the exclusive worship of God and obedience to God's ways—in short, justice and righteousness.

The immediate successors to the judges are Samuel and his sons. Indeed, 1 Samuel 7:15–17 suggests that Samuel was a judge; and 1 Samuel 8:1 tells us that Samuel "made his sons judges over Israel." But this arrangement does not work because Samuel's sons "perverted justice" (Hebrew *mišpaṭ;* 1 Sam. 8:3). This leads to the people's request for "a king to govern [Hebrew *špṭ*] us" (1 Sam. 8:5), a request that Samuel opposes but to which God reluctantly agrees, with the stipulation that Samuel "warn" the people about "the ways [Hebrew *mišpaṭ*!] of the king" (1 Sam. 8:9, 11). In short, the issue almost immediately after the book of Judges ends is again justice. Every attempt will be made to make the future monarchy a faithful institution. The kings are portrayed as sons of God (2 Sam. 7:14; Ps. 2:7) and are entrusted with enacting the justice and righteousness that God wills for the world (see Ps. 72:1–7; Jer. 22:1–16).

Thus, the judges occupy a place in the canonical sequence between Moses and Joshua, on the one hand, and the kings, on the other. It is this canonical position that has elevated local tribal chieftans or military heroes into "bringers of justice" in a broader sense (see below, section 2b). To be sure, this shift reflects the interests and commitments of the editors of the book, probably the Deuteronomistic Historians, who lent a form of unity to Israel's story using covenant as a central, organizing concept (see below, section 2c). Not surprisingly, both of the book's introductions (1:1—2:5; 2:6—3:6) mention "covenant" (2:1–2, 20); and the second virtually equates disobedience to the judges (2:17) with disobedience to God (2:20). The judges were cast in the role of covenant mediators in the final form of the book in its present canonical sequence (see below, section 3). They are thus portrayed as "bringers of justice," advocates of the exclusive worship of God and allegiance to God's ways.

A distinction is sometimes made between the so-called "major judges" (Othniel, Ehud, Deborah, Gideon, Jephthah, Samson) and the so-called "minor judges" (Shamgar, 3:31; Tola, 10:1–2; Jair, 10:3–5; Ibzan, 12:8–10; Elon, 12:11; Abdon, 12:13–15). Because Othniel is said to have "judged," and because Tola is involved in deliverance, it is difficult to maintain any functional distinction between the major and minor judges. The obvious distinction is the amount of material allotted. If Abimelech (chap. 9) is not counted as a judge, then the total number of judges is twelve. It seems likely that the compilers of the book incorporated the brief material about the so-called minor judges in order to attain this number, and perhaps also to achieve a more or less complete representation of all the tribes in the role of judging (see below, section 2c, as well as the commentary on 10:1–5 and 12:8–15).

2b. The Period(s) of the Judges

Until relatively recently, most critical biblical scholars were willing to speak of "the period of the judges," which was generally dated from about 1200–1020 B.C. According to this earlier consensus, the exodus took place about 1280 B.C., and the conquest of the land occurred about 1250–1200. Having taken control of the land, the people of Israel then supposedly formed a "tribal league" (see Josh. 24); and the judges were viewed as the leaders of this organization. They battled external enemies when necessary, and they exercised a loose administrative leadership during the intervals when "the land had rest" (Judg. 3:11, 30; 5:31; 8:28).

5

In recent years, however, biblical scholarship has revealed that the so-called conquest was a much more complex event than is suggested in the book of Joshua. In fact, one of the key sources in reaching this conclusion is Judges 1:1—2:5, which reports that many of the cities and territories supposedly taken by Joshua remained in Canaanite hands. This textual evidence, accompanied by archaeological findings and new anthropological studies, dictated the conclusion that the book of Joshua is a highly stylized account. And, it was recognized, so is the book of Judges. Its arrangement does not amount to even a roughly chronological account of actual events, and so it is highly misleading to speak of "the period of the judges." Rather, the material in the book of Judges has been ordered for theological purposes by editors who worked hundreds of years after the period from 1200 to 1020 B.C. In short, the so-called "period of the judges" was probably the creation of a person or persons known as the Deuteronomistic Historian (see below, section 2c).

To be sure, these editors were using older material that they had at their disposal; and to be sure, something happened in Canaan between the years 1200 and 1020. Indeed, it is likely that the stories found in the book of Judges originated well before the establishment of the monarchy in 1020. And it is likely that Othniel, Ehud, Deborah, Gideon, Jephthah, and Samson were local heroes whose exploits were remembered, passed on, and embellished over the years. Plus, the details in the lists of minor judges actually have a ring of historical authenticity to them, suggesting too that Shamgar, Tola, Jair, Ibzan, Elon, and Abdon may have been actual persons. What is not likely is that any of the judges, major or minor, actually delivered or governed all Israel as the book of Judges now suggests. Rather, as indicated above, the present arrangement addresses the issues and serves the theological purposes of a later time or times.

It is not surprising, therefore, that recent historians of premonarchical Israel paint a very different picture than the one portrayed by the book of Judges. In particular, premonarchical Israel is often described as a radically egalitarian society, in which women and men working together in small family units managed to squeeze out a subsistence-level existence in the hill country of Canaan at the margins of the territories controlled by the more powerful, established, and hierarchically organized Canaanite city-states. This portrait, or major aspects of it, may well be historically accurate. It accords well with the situation described in Judges 1:1—2:5; and it would serve to explain, for instance, how a woman like Deborah, who is both a prophet and a judge, could play a major administrative and religious role in the life of early Israel (Judg. 4:4–5). The song of Deborah and Barak is usually considered to be among the most ancient pieces of the Old Testament; and it, along with the some of the stories in the book of Judges, probably did actually originate in premonarchical Israel, about which the book of Judges purports to tell.

The problem with the contemporary reconstruction of premonarchical Israel is that it bears little resemblance to the actual book of Judges. To be sure, it is interesting and helpful; and the following commentary will make reference to what we know of the historical and cultural realities of premonarchic Israel. However, primary attention will be paid to the final form of the book of Judges. As suggested above, it is the compiler(s) and/or editor(s) of the book of Judges who arranged older material to create "the period of the judges." The work of the compiler(s) and/or editor(s) may have spanned several centuries; and from this perspective, it is more accurate to speak of "the *periods* of the judges." Thus, in the following commentary, consideration will be given to how the book of Judges, or portions of it, may have been shaped to address Israel and/or Judah during the monarchy, Judah during the late preexilic era, and the people of the exile and the restoration following the exile.

If there is any significant point of contact between the current historical reconstruction of premonarchical Israel and the actual book of Judges, it is that both portray Israel in a liminal situation. The English word "liminal" is derived from a Latin word that means "threshold," "border," or "margin"; and it is used to describe a person or situation that is in transition or "in between" more settled positions or stable moments. In the current historical reconstruction of premonarchic Israel, Israel is portrayed as liminal in the sense that it existed in the central highlands of Canaan on the borders, margins, or fringes of more desirable areas controlled by Canaanite city-states. It literally lived "in between" the more settled spheres of Canaanite control. In the book of Judges, Israel is "in between" the leadership of Moses and Joshua, heroes from the past, and the rise of a more permanent and settled institution, the future monarchy. In particular, the final five chapters of the book of Judges seem to anticipate the arrival of more settled leadership, by way of the recurring observation that, "In those days there was no king in Israel; all the people did what was right in their own eyes" (17:6; 21:25; see 18:1; 19:1).

Insofar as both the current historical reconstruction of premonarchic Israel and the book of Judges itself portray a liminal situation, they converge, perhaps, in suggesting that the challenge of covenant loyalty is the enduring challenge facing the people of God in every generation. In any case, as suggested above, this volume will attend primarily to the

7

final literary shape of the book of Judges, as well as the significance of the final form, thus relativizing (although not ignoring) the importance of historical reconstructions and conclusions.

2c. The Formation and Shape of the Book of Judges

As suggested above, much of the material in Judges probably dates originally from the years 1200 to 1020, the period in which the book of Judges purports to be set. But it is clear that this ancient material has been reworked, supplemented, and arranged, probably multiple times. The process of collecting the stories of local tribal heroes may have begun relatively early, and so may the process of shaping them for a particular purpose. For instance, the tribe of Judah is given preeminence throughout the book of Judges, beginning in 1:1—2:5. This would, of course, make sense in a variety of later historical contexts. For instance, it could have offered support for the Davidic monarchy and its claims, or reflected the historical reality that the southern kingdom outlasted the northern kingdom. When this is combined with the observation that portions of the book of Judges reflect very poorly on Benjamin and Gibeah (see especially chaps. 19—21), both associated with King Saul, it is possible to suppose that the earliest shaping of the material in Judges was intended to serve as political propaganda for the claims of David over Saul.

Be that as it may, it is likely that a much more definitive shaping of the ancient material took place several hundred years after the time of David. One of the most influential and enduring theories from the history of biblical scholarship in the twentieth century is Martin Noth's proposal for the existence of a Deuteronomistic History. Noth suggested that persons schooled in the perspective contained in the book of Deuteronomy shaped ancient traditions, sources, and stories to create a more or less unified narrative that includes the books of Deuteronomy, Joshua, Judges, 1 and 2 Samuel, and 1 and 2 Kings. It is not precisely clear who these Deuteronomistic Historians were, nor exactly when, where, and how long they worked. Noth's theory has been refined, modified, and expanded by many scholars; and it now appears most likely that the Deuteronomistic History originated not long after the fall of the northern kingdom in 722 B.C. It probably went through several "editions," the last of which reflects the experience of the destruction of Jerusalem in 587 B.C., the subsequent exile, and perhaps the restoration (or at least the hope of restoration).

8   The Deuteronomistic Historians were committed to the exclusive worship of the one God of Israel in the one place, Jerusalem. They vested considerable hope in the Davidic monarchy, although they were

quite aware of its shortcomings and attempted to hold it to the highest and strictest of standards (see Deut. 17:14–20). Indeed, the Deuteronomistic Historians suggested that the eventual destruction of Jerusalem, the loss of the monarchy, and the subsequent exile were to be explained by the failure of the people, and especially the monarchs, to respond obediently to the torah itself, and to the prophetic call to embody the justice and righteousness that the torah demands (see 2 Kgs. 17:7–20). Even so, the retributional scheme contained in the book of Deuteronomy (in chaps. 27—30, the blessings and curses that are to result from obeying or disobeying the torah), and in the Deuteronomistic History, is actually subverted by the Deuteronomistic History itself, which ends by offering at least the hint that God was not finished with God's people, including even the monarchy (see 2 Kgs. 25:27–30). In commenting on the final four verses of 2 Kings, Richard Nelson writes:

> Kings concludes with God's options held wide open. In this, the book is a paradigm of all biblical faith. The key to the future lies with God alone. The experience of both Israel and the church testifies that the God of the Bible is the God of surprise happy endings and amazing grace. (Nelson, 269)

In short, the Deuteronomistic Historians at least hint that God will ultimately be gracious. (See also Barry G. Webb, 209; Webb articulates this view, pointing out that the book of Judges itself contains anything but "a mechanical theory of history" by way of its portrayal of God's "contrariness-to-expectation," including the showing of mercy). This direction was picked up by exilic and postexilic prophets (see Isa. 40—66); and the ideal of the Davidic monarchy remained alive long after its historical demise, in the form of the conviction either that the people as a whole had become the successors to David's line, or that the Davidic line would eventually be restored.

As suggested above, it is the Deuteronomistic Historians who were responsible for creating "the period of the judges." The clearest evidence of their work is found in Judg. 2:6—3:6, which includes the basic framework that recurs throughout the book of Judges and that provides a unity among the various stories of the individual judges. The cycle contains the following elements:

1. The people do "evil" by worshiping Baal and other gods (2:11–13; see also 3:7, 12; 4:1; 6:1; 10:6; 13:1).
2. God is angry at the people's faithlessness and allows them to be oppressed by their enemies (2:14–15; see also 3:8, 12–14; 4:2; 6:1–5; 10:7–10; 13:1).

9

3. God raises up a judge/deliverer in response to the people's crying out for help (see 2:18, where the "groaning" of the people is mentioned rather than their crying out; see also 3:9, 15; 4:3–10; 6:6–18; 10:10–16). The oppression is relieved, and there is stability as long as the judge lives.
4. The judge dies; the people turn again to idolatry and disobedience; and the cycle begins again (see 2:19).

The nature of the cycle would have served well the purposes of the Deuteronomistic Historians in both the preexilic and exilic/postexilic eras. In the former, the cycle would have functioned as a warning to the people that disobedience will have destructive consequences, as the individual prophets also warned the people. In the latter, the cycle would have functioned to offer the hope and promise that God hears oppressed people when they cry out for help, as the individual prophetic books in their final forms also proclaim. In short, the cycle would have functioned both to offer an explanation for the exile and to hold out the possibility of hope beyond destruction.

A careful reading of the book of Judges reveals that the cycle is not fully represented in each case. More specifically, the cycle becomes more disjointed or incomplete as the book progresses. For instance, the people's cry in 10:10 is a confession of sin rather than a cry for help. This would seem to be a good sign, but God responds by saying, "I will deliver you no more" (10:13). Actually, Jephthah does proceed to defeat the Ammonites, but his victory is flawed by his tragic vow. By the time we get to Samson, the pattern has almost fallen apart. The people do not cry out, and we are told that Samson will only "begin to deliver Israel from the hand of the Philistines" (13:5).

After the story of Samson, the cycle disappears completely. While chapters 17—21 are often seen as a late addition to the book of Judges, or as an epilogue, they really offer a very logical conclusion to the direction that chapters 3—16 have taken. Things have been progressively falling apart, and in chapters 17—21 the breakdown is complete. Idols are manufactured and worshiped; priests are for hire. The murder of one woman leads to a bloody civil war, in which the tribe of Benjamin is nearly wiped out. When there is an attempt to make amends, further atrocities occur. In short, moral confusion and social chaos were the order of the day, because "there was no king in Israel; all the people did what was right in their own eyes" (21:25; see 17:6; 18:1; 19:1).

10

On the surface, chapters 17—21—and indeed the progressive deterioration that occurs throughout the book of Judges—seem to be a none-too-subtle setup for the Davidic monarchy. In fact, it is likely that the book of Judges was shaped with this purpose in mind. As suggested above, the Deuteronomistic Historians generally supported the monarchy; and a preexilic edition of the Deuteronomistic History may well have been aimed at using "the period of the judges" to make a case for the legitimacy of the monarchy.

If so, however, it is necessary to recall the likelihood that an exilic or postexilic "edition" of the Deuteronomistic History was produced. From the perspective of the exile, it appeared that the monarchy, like the office of the judge, had failed. The message contained in this failure is that no institution—not even the Davidic monarchy—is exempt from the consequences of idolatry and unfaithfulness. The historical fact of the failure and disappearance of the Davidic monarchy is crucial for the interpretation of the book of Judges.

It means, for instance, that the book of Judges cannot simply be read as Davidic propaganda, even though it may have served as such at one time in its history. Nor can the book of Judges be read triumphally as it has sometimes been read by both Jews and Christians (see below, section 3b). When God's people and their institutions fail to facilitate the exclusive worship of God and fail to embody God's will, *they too* will suffer the destructive consequences that result from idolatry and disobedience.

What seemed to grow out of the disaster of exile was the awareness that God shows no partiality. Idolatry and disobedience will destroy God's people as they will destroy any people. But what also grew out of the exile was a new or renewed awareness that the God of Israel is also the God of all peoples, all nations, and indeed all creation. This universal God, it was realized, can do nothing other than will to gather a universal people. So, if Israel/Judah has a special role, it will involve somehow being a blessing to "all the families of the earth" (Gen. 12:3) and "a light to the nations" (Isa. 42:6). Israel's privilege is the privilege of servanthood. God's city, therefore, is not simply the place for Israel/Judah to gather. Rather, it will be a gathering place for "all the nations" (Isa. 2:2). Israel's land, which is the object of contention in the books of Joshua and Judges, becomes, in essence, the property of all the nations! Ultimately, this is what God wills for the world. Indeed, the gathering of all the nations will show that God "will establish justice among the nations" (Isa. 2:4, my trans.).

What all this means is that the book of Judges must be read, not only against the backdrop of the historical circumstances in which its stories originated, not only against the backdrop of the historical circumstances in which its material was compiled and edited, and not only

11

with a careful eye toward the final form of the book itself. It must also finally be read and interpreted as part of the whole canonical story contained in the Torah and the Prophets, a story that begins in Genesis and ends with a forgiven and restored people who are commissioned and positioned to be "a light to the nations."

3. The Book of Judges in the Context of the Canon

Although it is often argued that the exodus is the crucial event of the Old Testament, it is extraordinarily important that Israel chose to tell its authoritative story beginning with creation, thus affirming that its God is the God of all humankind and all creation. As Terence Fretheim has convincingly demonstrated, the exodus narrative and the book of Exodus are only comprehensible in the light of Genesis (Fretheim, Exodus, 12–22). The exodus and the giving of the torah aim at the fulfillment of God's creational purposes, a world in which humanity can live and thrive without death-dealing institutions and policies like those of Pharaoh. In the book of Genesis, even when the narrative narrows its focus from all the nations to Abraham and Sarah and their descendants (Gen. 12:1–3), the blessing of Abraham is to involve somehow the blessing of "all the families of the earth" (Gen. 12:3).

Not only is it extraordinarily important that the Torah begins with creation, but it is also critically important that it ends with the book of Deuteronomy. This is an unnatural division, it would seem, because it interrupts the story before the promise to the ancestors is fulfilled in the book of Joshua. But, as James Sanders has suggested, this unnatural division was almost certainly quite intentional (Sanders, 1–53). Its effect is to leave the Torah, Israel's most authoritative body of Scripture, severed from possession of the land. Thus, Israel's most authoritative body of Scripture leaves the people perpetually *outside* the land. This, of course, accurately reflects the experience of exilic/postexilic Israel, which never really controlled the land again after 587 B.C. The concluding of the Torah with Deuteronomy was actually a brilliant move that opened the way for the creation of Judaism in the postexilic era and for the existence of Judaism as a world religion rather than simply a regional religion tied inextricably to the land of Canaan.

To be sure, the Former Prophets (the books of Joshua, Judges, 1 and 2 Samuel, and 1 and 2 Kings) narrate Israel's entry into and possession of the land, but they also narrate Israel's loss of the land with the defeats of Samaria in 722 B.C. and Jerusalem in 587 B.C. The Latter Prophets (Isaiah, Jeremiah, Ezekiel, the Book of the Twelve) attempt to come to terms with this reality, both by providing an "explanation" for it (the people's failure to worship God alone and to do God's will) and by projecting a future beyond the destruction. The first book of the Latter Prophets, Isaiah, is especially influential. Its concluding chapters proclaim God's forgiveness of the people (40:1–2), anticipate their return to the land, and position them as the servant of a universal God whose sovereignty is still in effect (Isa. 52:7–10). This God wills nothing less than that God's people be "a light to the nations" (Isa. 42:6; 49:6) in order to effect God's will "to establish justice among the nations" (Isa. 2:4). (See Isa. 42:4, where the mission of the servant is to "bring forth justice to the nations," and note the repetition of "justice" in vv. 3–4.)

Klaus Koch has aptly described the theology of the Latter Prophets as "ethical futuristic monotheism," the anthropological correlate of which he calls "concentric monanthropology" (Koch, 12–14). In other words, because the prophets proclaim the one universal God who rules all the nations, there must be in this God's sight a single humanity—one God, one humanity. This God can will nothing other than "justice among the nations" (Isa. 2:2), "justice in the earth" (Isa. 42:4), because the whole world belongs to this God. Thus, the convergence between the perspective of the Prophets, the second portion of the Jewish canon, and the Torah, the first portion of the Jewish canon, is clear: The Torah begins with a portrayal of a universal creator, and the Prophets offer a portrayal of a sovereign God whose will is not complete until "all the ends of the earth shall see the salvation [that is, the life-giving power] of our God" (Isa. 52:10).

This convergence seems more clear, however, between the Torah and the *Latter* Prophets, like Isaiah, which initiates the collection. What about the *Former* Prophets, including the book of Judges (along with Joshua and 1 Samuel through 2 Kings), in which God does *not* appear to be so universalistic, but rather seems to favor Israel over against other peoples and nations, and to do so rather violently at times? It is this very question, in one form or another, that seems most frequently to plague contemporary readers of the book of Judges (see above, section 1).

The context of the canon offers some perspective on this genuinely troubling question. Above all, it suggests that the book of Judges should finally be heard in the context of the material that surrounds it—that is, both the Torah with its portrayal of a God who creates and claims the whole world, and the Latter Prophets with its congruent portrayal of an ultimate sovereign whose purposes encompass all nations. In short, nothing in the book of Judges should be construed as a contradiction of God's universal sovereignty and God's will for justice and righteousness   13 among all the peoples of the earth.

When the Former Prophets, including the book of Judges, are

indeed heard in their larger canonical context, they actually highlight a crucial feature of God's sovereign work—namely, that the universal God works particularistically. In other words, the particular people, Israel, is to play a crucial role in the fulfillment of God's world-encompassing will. The crucial question is this: Will Israel be faithful to God alone so that it fulfills its God-given role? Indeed, this is the crucial question that is posed at the very beginning of the book of Judges (see commentary on 1:1—2:5; 2:6—3:6) and that pervades the whole book. And this question inevitably leads to another: When Israel fails to be faithful, how will God respond?

Actually, of course, both of these questions have already been posed within the Torah itself. As the book of Exodus unfolds, God's primary opponent proves to be not Pharaoh and his death-dealing policies, but rather God's own recently liberated people and their propensity to disobey. Almost immediately following the covenant ceremony in which the people promise twice to obey God (see Exod. 24:1–11, especially vv. 3, 7), they in fact prove to be grossly disobedient, choosing idolatry, the worship of a golden calf, instead of faithfulness to God (Exod. 32:1–6). To be sure, the people thereby invoked God's wrath (Exod. 32:7–10), but following Moses' intercession for the people (Exod. 32:11–13) God "changed his mind about the disaster that he planned to bring on his people" (Exod. 32:14). The conclusion to the golden calf episode presents God as "merciful and gracious, slow to anger, and abounding in steadfast love and faithfulness, . . . forgiving iniquity and transgression and sin, yet by no means clearing the guilty" (Exod. 34:6–7).

In a real sense, the books of Joshua and Judges involve a replaying of the sequence found in the book of Exodus. The crossing of the Jordan in Joshua 3:14—4:24 recalls the crossing of the sea and the exodus from Egypt in Exodus 14. The subsequent defeat of the people of the land (Josh. 6—12) parallels the defeat of Pharaoh and his army in the book of Exodus; and not surprisingly, the circumcision of the wilderness generation in Joshua 5 rather clearly alludes to the golden calf episode when its effect is described as having "rolled away from you the disgrace of Egypt" (Josh. 5:9). As in the book of Exodus, deliverance leads to covenant; and Joshua 24, the book's final chapter, specifically recalls Exodus 24 and its covenant ceremony.

Thus, as the book of Judges begins, the newly delivered and constituted people have a renewed opportunity to worship and serve God alone (see Josh. 24:14–16; Judg 1:1—2:5). As if to go one better than their ancestors in Exodus 24, the newly delivered people in Joshua 24 promise *three* times to serve God alone (vv. 18, 21, 24). But will they?

14

As suggested above, it is precisely this question that initiates and pervades the book of Judges.

In a word, of course, the answer is *no*. From the very beginning of the book of Judges, the people assert their own will over against God's will (see commentary on 1:1—2:5); and they worship the Baals of the land instead of God alone (see commentary on 2:6—3:6). And what's more, they do these things *repeatedly* throughout the book of Judges. Each deliverance recounted in the book of Judges amounts to a sort of new exodus (or at least a new mini-exodus), and each is followed eventually by the people's unfaithful response. But God delivers *again and again*. (See above, section 2c, for a description of the repeated cycle or pattern that unifies the book of Judges.) Thus, in a real sense the book of Judges actually involves *multiple replayings* of the pattern found already in the Torah, especially the book of Exodus: God delivers the people, who then disobey, experiencing not only the destructive results of their disobedience (the guilty are by no means cleared, as Exod. 34:7 says) but also the steadfast love and faithfulness of a God who cannot finally let the people go (see below, section 4).

This pattern in the book of Judges, however, not only recalls the book of Exodus; it also anticipates the subsequent books of the Former Prophets, as well as the Latter Prophets. Finally, Israel's persistent idolatry and disobedience lead to the apparent rupture of the relationship, as the Former Prophets recount (in 2 Kings), and as the Latter Prophets have warned. But when it seems that the covenant has been abrogated forever, the conclusion of the Former Prophets (2 Kgs. 25) holds out a glimmer of hope; and the Latter Prophets, especially the book of Isaiah, proclaim that a forgiving God has effected yet another new exodus, this time in the form of a return from exile (see especially Isa. 40—55; and see above, section 2c). The pattern found in the book of Exodus and replayed several times in the book of Judges is still in effect.

The connections between the book of Judges and its canonical context are important. They serve to remind the reader that the book of Judges *is* one of the prophetic books. By highlighting the question: Will Israel worship and serve God alone? the book of Judges joins the other prophetic books in calling the people of God in every generation to covenant faithfulness—the worship of God alone and the pursuit of the justice, righteousness, and peace that God wills. Like the other prophetic books, the book of Judges, by way of its portrayal of the destructive consequences of idolatry and disobedience, serves as a warning. But also like the other prophetic books, the warning is grounded in the hope that the God of Israel will ultimately be faithful to even a persistently unfaithful people (see above, section 1; and see below, section 4).

Then too, the connections between the book of Judges and its canonical context affect the way that major aspects of the book of Judges are to be heard and understood. In other words, from a Reformed perspective at least, the whole of Scripture affects the interpretation of specific parts. So, we turn now to a consideration of how the canonical context of the book of Judges has an impact on major interpretive features of the book.

3a. The Land

Victor H. Matthews sums up admirably how God's dispersed people in the postexilic era came to view the land of Canaan: "Having a 'promised land' no longer meant simply Canaan/Palestine/Israel. Rather, it was broadened to mean wherever they lived as members of the covenant community" (Matthews, *Old Testament Themes*, 38). Such a broadening of perspective is entirely in keeping with the prophetic views that developed in the exilic and postexilic eras. Israel's land, and more specifically, Jerusalem, the former capital of Judah, is to be a gathering place for all the nations as a sign of God's will for the establishment of justice among all nations and to the ends of the earth (Isa. 2:1–4; 52:7–10).

To be sure, the book of Judges narrates an extended struggle over the land of Canaan/Palestine/Israel. But, when the book of Judges is read in the context of the larger canonical story of which it is a part, the reader is invited and encouraged to understand land symbolically. In biblical terms, land represents access to life. During the years 1200 to 1020 Canaan was in the process of becoming an agrarian society, which it remained throughout the years of the monarchy (although it became a more advanced agrarian society with directions toward urbanization and the development of a market economy). In an agrarian society one must have land in order to have a future—in short, to live. This is why the book of Joshua bothers to list the allotment of land, not just for every tribe, but also in some cases to every family of a tribe (Josh. 13:8—21:45). This is also why it was such a grievous thing for Naboth to lose his family inheritance (1 Kgs. 21:1–16). Everyone needed land. It was a matter of justice and righteousness; or in other words, it was a matter of the fulfillment of God's creational purposes that humanity live and thrive. In Naboth's case, the prophet Elijah got involved (1 Kgs. 21:17–29). From a canonical perspective, the prophets are simultaneously advocates of justice and righteousness, spokespersons for God, and proclaimers of torah. But, of course, all these things go hand-in-

16

hand. What God wills and teaches (torah means essentially "instruction," not "law") is the creation of conditions that make life possible for humankind.

As suggested above, the book of Judges is part of the prophetic canon. When the book of Judges is heard as a prophetic word in its context, within the story that begins in Genesis and concludes with the Latter Prophets, then the theological issue at stake in the struggle for land is whether and how life will be possible. According to the book of Judges, life is possible, but only within a faithful relationship to the one God of Israel—that is, only when Israel honors its covenant promises to worship God alone and to pursue God's ways exclusively. Only when Israel is faithful can it possibly effect a blessing for "all the families of the earth" (Gen. 12:3) and serve as "a light to the nations" (Isa. 42:6; 49:6). It is the role of the judges to enact the conditions that make covenant life possible, including opposition to oppressive enemies and leadership in the direction of the worship and service of God alone.

The opposite of faithful relationship to Israel's God is idolatry and self-assertion, which actually amount to the same thing. By obliterating Israel's covenant identity, idolatry and self-assertion endanger Israel's possessing of the land—that is, they endanger life. To understand this more fully, and to appreciate how idolatry and self-assertion are really the same thing, we move to a consideration of the Canaanites and what they represent in the book of Judges.

3b. The Canaanites

The failure to understand Israel's relationship to the Canaanites in the context of the larger canonical story that begins in Genesis and continues throughout the Torah and the Prophets has meant that the book of Judges has often been used by Christian interpreters to legitimate violence rather than to pursue God's creational purposes. For instance, Puritan preachers in colonial North America suggested that the indigenous peoples were to be viewed as Canaanites while the Christian English settlers were the successors of the Israelites—God's New Israel. Then, appealing to the book of Judges, the Puritan preachers concluded that the land of the indigenous peoples was to be appropriated, and that they were to be either converted or wiped out. It is a tragic story; and indeed, the violence on which the United States of America was founded is still a pervasive feature of life in this country and throughout the world. While many contemporary folk are apt to criticize the book of Judges for being excessively violent, they fail to realize that the twentieth century was far and away the most violent century in the history of humankind.

17

This fact, along with a history of abuse based in part on readings of the book of Judges, makes it crucial to arrive at an understanding of the Canaanites that is based on a reading of the book of Judges in its larger canonical context. Noting the use of the book of Judges to sanction violence against Native Americans, Robert Allen Warrior reaches the following important conclusions:

> First, the Canaanites should be at the center of Christian theological reflection and political action. . . . Keeping the Canaanites at the center makes it more likely that those who read the Bible will read *all* of it, not just the part that inspires and justifies them. (Warrior, 264)

As stated above in the discussion of the land in the book of Judges, the larger canonical context is crucial.

When the book of Judges is read apart from the larger canonical context, it can be (and has been) understood to mean that God plays favorites. In short, God only loves God's "chosen people"; and these "chosen people" are rewarded by God at the expense of other people—Canaanites, Egyptians, and so on. To be sure, various groups at various points in history have identified themselves as the exclusively chosen ones—ancient Israelites and Judeans, later Jews, Christians throughout the centuries, and some modern Israelis. And, on the basis of their chosenness, and allegedly in keeping with the book of Judges, these folk have persecuted and killed those whom they have identified as "the Canaanites." Jews have killed Muslims; Christians have killed Jews, Muslims, Native Americans, and Africans; and contemporary Israelis and Palestinian Christians and Muslims are often willing to kill each other. Each of these groups in various times and places have ignored the Bible's witness to a God who claims all humanity as God's own, who wills justice, righteousness, and peace among all nations, and who, when designating any particular people as "chosen," wills them to be agents of a world-encompassing reign of justice, righteousness, and peace.

This God, the God revealed in the final form of the Torah and the Prophets (and, for Christians, in the New Testament and in Jesus), does not hate Canaanites or any other race, people, or nation. This God loves the world; and consequently, this God does not play favorites by ordering the slaughter of Canaanites so that God's alleged favorites can take their land. Thus, when it is heard in its larger canonical context, the book of Judges cannot be used to legitimate violence. This means that the references to the Canaanites (and other peoples named in the book of Judges as enemies of Israel) must be understood symbolically.

In this regard, it is helpful again to compare the book of Judges to the book of Exodus. As Terence Fretheim argues, when God opposes

18

Pharaoh in the book of Exodus, it is not because God hates Egyptians and favors Israelites, but rather because Pharaoh represents the forces of death. As an agent of oppression and death, Pharaoh was thwarting God's *creational* purposes, God's will for life for humankind. Similarly, in the book of Judges, God's opposition to the Canaanites should not be understood to mean God's hatred of a particular people; rather, it indicates God's opposition to a way of life that was based on injustice and unrighteousness that consequently resulted in deadly oppression. As E. John Hamlin points out:

> "Canaanites" in Judg. 1 is a kind of code word referring to those forces, structures, and individuals who were seen to be in opposition to the good order of Yahweh. The real adversary was not a whole people, but a way of organizing society. (Hamlin, 14)

J. P. M. Walsh's analysis of the Baalism of the Canaanite system may be instructive at this point, although admittedly it is based on material beyond the book of Judges and is an interpretive construal. Walsh argues that Baalism, the religion of the Canaanites, elevated survival above compassion, whereas Yahwism put compassion above survival. In essence, the worship of fertility gods and goddesses like the Baals and Asherahs was an attempt to manipulate divinity to serve the human need for agricultural productivity season after season. To be sure, human survival and the attendant need for productivity are understandable motivations (and ones to which many forms of Christianity have historically conformed and still conform); but they are based on putting divinity at human disposal. In short, from this perspective, idolatry (worshiping Baal) and self-assertion (putting God at human disposal) become synonymous. According to Walsh, any system that makes human need, even the need for survival, an ultimate concern, inevitably results in an hierarchically organized society in which the more successful producers dominate the less successful ones. Biblical examples would include Pharaoh's Egypt, as well as the Canaanite city-state system (Walsh, 13–28).

When references to "the Canaanites" are heard symbolically as references to ways of organizing social life that perpetuate injustice and ultimately produce oppressive inequalities that threaten human life, then the book of Judges will not be heard as justification for any "chosen" group to take the land and/or resources of others. Nor will the book of Judges be understood to sanction genocide or any other forms of violence. Rather, the book of Judges will be heard as a prophetic call to establish the justice, righteousness, and peace that are willed by a God who has compassion for all humanity.

. Given the tragic history of the use of the book of Judges to sanction violent self-interest, it is pertinent to recall at this point not only the canonical context of the book of Judges, but also the shape of the book itself, especially its pattern of progressive deterioration (see above, section 2c). As the book unfolds, it is increasingly reminiscent of the book of Exodus, in which the problem finally was not Pharaoh and Egypt but rather the idolatrous and disobedient Israelites (see Exod. 32—34). So too, in the book of Judges, the primary problem is not so much the Canaanites as it is the Israelites themselves! They are self-assertive and idolatrous from the very beginning (see commentary on 1:1—2:5; 2:6—3:6). By the end of the book, the utter chaos is marked by Israelite-on-Israelite violence that nearly decimates the tribe of Benjamin.

From this perspective, the book of Judges was an invitation to ancient Israel, and it is an invitation to God's people in every generation, to set its own house in order—that is, to worship and serve God alone—rather than violently posturing itself as superior to, or more deserving than, others (whoever the others are perceived to be). In short, to follow the canonical clues to interpret "the Canaanites" symbolically may well mean to hear the book of Judges—as other prophetic books are usually more readily heard—as a call to repentance, which in turn may serve as an impetus for God's people to join in the fulfillment of God's creational purposes for humankind.

Then too, from this perspective the book of Judges illustrates the profound difficulty of worshiping and serving God alone amid the persistent human propensity for idolatry/self-assertion (that is, sin!), as well as the disastrously destructive consequences of failing to embody God's creational purposes for the world. Perhaps, from this perspective, one might even say that the book of Judges is finally testimony to the God who violently wills peace—an oxymoron that invites attention to the function of violence and vengeance in the book of Judges.

3c. Violence and Vengeance

The previous sections have touched on the characteristics that most persons associate most readily with the book of Judges when they say that the book is full of violence and portrays God as wrathful and vengeful. To be sure, there are violent stories in the book of Judges. One of the problems, however, when contemporary persons point to the excessive violence in the book of Judges is their implication that *we* live in a *less* violent world. In fact, as suggested above, the twentieth century was by far the most violent century in human history; and violence is a daily staple of life in the United States of America—in homes, in schools, in neighborhoods, on ball fields, not to mention television and movies. In fact, if it were heard in its final form and within its larger canonical context, the book of Judges might serve as a timely reminder to us of *our* violent ways. In short, the book of Judges is not a commendation of violence but rather a condemnation of it. It reminds its readers that when God's justice, righteousness, and peace are not established for all, then violence is the natural result.

As in the exodus story, the violence in the book of Judges serves the purpose of fulfilling God's creational purposes. In the book of Exodus, the Israelites were already the victims of Pharaoh's violent policies. Egyptians die in the story, not because God wills their destruction but rather because they persist in perpetuating deadly injustice. In essence, those who lived by the sword died by the sword. If Pharaoh had quit enslaving and killing Israelites—that is, if Pharaoh had abided by God's will—the cycle of violence would have been broken. The book of Exodus, therefore, is a realistic reminder that oppressors seldom, if ever, give up without a fight. Because oppression is simply institutionalized violence, God "fights" back. If this is wrath, it is righteous wrath. If this is vengeance, it is vengeance in the service of God's creational purposes for humankind.

What applies to the book of Exodus also applies to the book of Judges. Insofar as God can be described as wrathful or vengeful, God's anger is righteous indignation, and God's vengeance aims at the establishment of justice, righteousness, and peace in situations of deadly oppression. In those portions of the book of Judges where the violence is random and excessive (for instance, chaps. 17—21), the book itself suggests that such violence is the result of idolatry, faithlessness, and injustice. Thus, the book functions at these points as a warning against idolatry and disobedience, and hence as a call to repentance. As suggested above (in section 2c), the book in its final form demonstrates a pattern of progressive deterioration; and it is precisely this pattern that is the primary means by which the book serves as a condemnation of idolatry and disobedience and their inevitably violent and destructive consequences. A major indicator of the pattern of progressive deterioration is the changing role of the female characters in the book of Judges.

3d. The Role of Women

There are numerous female characters in the book of Judges, at least twenty-two individuals or groups of women: Achsah (1:11–15); Deborah (chaps. 4—5); Jael (4:17–23; 5:4–27); the mother of Sisera (5:28); her "wisest ladies" (5:29–30); Gideon's concubine, the mother of

Abimelech (8:31; 9:1–3); "a certain woman" (9:53), who kills Abimelech; Jephthah's mother (11:1); Gilead's wife (11:2–3); Jephthah's daughter (11:34–40); the companions of Jephthah's daughter (11:37–38); "the daughters of Israel" (11:44); Samson's mother, the wife of Manoah (13:2–25); Samson's wife from Timnah (14:1—15:8); the prostitute whom Samson visited in Gaza (16:1–3); Delilah (16:4–22); the women of the Philistines (16:27); Micah's mother (17:1–6); the Levite's concubine (19:1–30); the "virgin daughter" of the Levite's host at Gibeah (19:24); the "four hundred young virgins" of Jabesh-gilead (21:12); and "the young women of Shiloh" (21:21).

To be sure, some of these are minor characters; however, no less than ten of the female characters have speaking parts. Although neither of them speaks, the "certain woman" kills Abimelech, the would-be king, and the Levite's concubine receives major attention. And, of course, Deborah is one of the judges, although the actual deliverance in chapters 4—5 is effected by Jael, another woman.

The major place occupied by women in the book of Judges is surprising, given the patriarchal orientation of ancient Israelite society; however, it may not be as surprising as it first seems. For instance, the major role played by women in the book of Judges likely reflects the origin of the stories in premonarchic Israel, an era significantly more egalitarian than monarchic Israel would later become (see above, section 2b). In any case, what Susan Ackermann calls the "remarkable assembly of women and the multitude of roles they play in the book of Judges" has led to a proliferation of studies of the book from a feminist perspective. (See Ackermann, *Warrior, Dancer, Seductress, Queen: Women in Judges and Biblical Israel*, 6; in addition, see several of the essays in Yee, *Judges and Method;* Brenner, *A Feminist Companion to Judges;* and Fewell, "Judges," in *The Women's Bible Commentary.*)

Several of these studies will be cited later; for now, one study in particular suggests how the portrayal of women in the book of Judges highlights the pattern of progressive deterioration. Adrian Janis Bledstein considers the possibility that the major role of women in the book is to be explained by female authorship. She concludes:

> Read as a woman's satirical narrative, the book of Judges is a trenchant criticism of human (most often male) arrogance. We might imagine Huldah [whom Bledstein suggests may have been the Deuteronomist] designing this scroll to admonish the young monarch Josiah: "Beware of he-who-would-be-God." (Bledstein, 54)

Even if Bledstein is incorrect about the female authorship of the book of Judges or about Huldah being the Deuteronomist, her analysis is extremely helpful. Undoubtedly, women play supremely positive roles in the book, especially Achsah (1:11–15), Deborah, and Jael (chaps. 4–5); and clearly, the fortunes of women decline as the book of Judges proceeds. Jephthah's daughter is killed (11:34–40); the Levite's concubine is raped, killed, and dismembered (chap. 19); and the book ends with the abduction of the "four hundred young virgins" of Jabesh-gilead (21:12) and "the young women of Shiloh" (21:21). As the book of Judges proceeds, increasing injustice results in moral confusion and social chaos, a primary indication of which is the abuse of women. In the time of Josiah, and in our own time, the book of Judges serves as a call to repentance for injustices and abuses that result from unbridled self-assertion/idolatry—injustice and abuses that, then and now, often most directly affect women.

3e. Humor

Abuse and injustice are no laughing matter; however, humor in some form is often one of the few means of resistance for marginalized people. For instance, Bledstein's proposal to understand the book of Judges as a satirical narrative by women (see above, section 3d) illustrates how this particular form of humor might function in the book of Judges as a means of resistance.

There are other possibilities. Given the likelihood that many of the stories originated in the period of 1200 to 1020, when elements of Israel struggled against the more organized and powerful forces of the Canaanite city-state system, the humor in some of the stories may amount to an act of resistance by an oppressed group. The name of the king opposed by the first judge, Othniel, is clearly symbolic, and probably also meant to be humorous: Cushan-rishathaim, which means "Cushan of the Double Wickedness." The humor in the story of the second judge, Ehud (3:12–30), is literally what we call today "bathroom humor," still a staple of contemporary stand-up comedians who regularly get laughs by speaking crudely of bodily functions. Part of the original purpose may well have been to entertain, but the humor also communicates hopeful resistance by a clearly weaker force.

As the book of Judges proceeds and the spiral of progressive deterioration unfolds, the problem increasingly becomes internal and the role of humor shifts accordingly. To be sure, there is nothing the least bit funny in stories like those of Jephthah's daughter and the Levite's concubine, which Phyllis Trible has rightly called "texts of terror." But the story of Samson is another matter. It is at once tragic and humorous. Samson's riddle again involves the humor of bodily functions—vomiting, in this case, another staple of modern comedy. And Samson's reply to the men of Timnah when they "solve" his riddle once again features a constant of today's comedy—sex and ways to describe sexual intercourse. The humor in these instances seems intended primarily to entertain, but the humor in the story of Samson and Delilah has a more serious side. Delilah's behavior in the story is not exactly subtle. Everyone, including the reader, knows what Delilah is doing, except Samson, who is incredibly and ridiculously clueless. Herein lies both the tragedy and the humor; but of course, this time the joke is on Samson, Israel's judge. Thus, the humor in this case is not an act of resistance but rather an indication of Israel's inability to offer any resistance. With Samson, the deterioration is complete. Israel's only enemy in chapters 17—21 is itself as it moves nearly to self-annihilation. There is nothing to laugh about in these chapters. (See, however, Stuart Lasine, 43–50, who argues that the sheer ludicrousness of the events in Judges 17—21 is intended to be a form of absurd humor.)

4. Theology in the Book of Judges

The issue at the beginning of the book of Judges (and repeatedly throughout the book) is whether Israel will be faithful to the covenant. Will Israel worship and serve God alone? (See above, section 3.) Underlying this issue is the profound and fundamental theological claim that God alone is sovereign, and hence that the chief end of Israel is to honor, trust, and obey God alone.

This issue and its underlying claim can be (and is) stated in a variety of other ways in both the Old and the New Testament. For instance, will the people of God "have no other gods before" God (Exod. 20:3)? Or, will the people of God know that "The LORD is our God, the LORD alone"; and will they obey the command to "love the LORD your God with all your heart, and with all your soul, and with all your might" (Deut. 6:4–5)? The latter of these texts, the Shema, was cited by Jesus when he was asked, "Which commandment in the law is the greatest?" (Matt. 22:36), a reminder that Jesus' proclamation of the kingdom of God articulates the same fundamental theological claim that lies at the heart of the book of Judges—that God alone is sovereign.

Although Gideon specifically affirms God's sole sovereignty (by his words more than by his deeds; see Judg. 8:22–23 and the commentary on 8:4–35), the book of Judges is largely a rehearsal of the people's failure to worship and serve God alone. As for the judges themselves, beginning with Gideon, their leadership is increasingly questionable and ineffective; and the book of Judges ends in utter chaos (see above, section 2c, as well as the commentary on chaps. 17—21). Even so, by the end of the book of Judges, God has *repeatedly* delivered an unfaith-

24

ful people in what amounts to an unfolding series of new exoduses; and in the ongoing canonical narrative, God will continue to do so.

The cyclical pattern that unifies the book of Judges has extraordinary theological significance, suggesting, for instance, what kind of sovereignty Israel's God exercises (see commentary on 2:6—3:6). The sovereignty or power of Israel's God does not consist of sheer force or enforcement. If it did, God either should have been more successful in whipping Israel into shape, or God should have simply punished Israel incessantly. Instead, however, Israel's God in the book of Judges and throughout the Bible simply cannot and will not be unfaithful to an inveterately unfaithful people (see Judg. 2:18; 10:16). In short, God's sovereignty takes the form of steadfast love. Israel's God is essentially gracious and merciful (see Exod. 34:6–7).

But as the book of Judges demonstrates, God's grace is not cheap. God bears the brunt of the people's disobedience (see commentary on 10:6–16); and Israel repeatedly experiences the debilitating, destructive, deadly consequences of its idolatry and disobedience. In this sense, the guilty are by no means cleared (see Exod. 34:7); however, the guilty are by no means abandoned or condemned either. The repeated cycle of deliverances in the book of Judges portrays a God whose essential will is to forgive and give life (see Howard, 118–20; and Wilcock, 13–16).

By fully documenting the disastrous consequences of idolatry and disobedience, the book of Judges amply demonstrates its prophetic character. As part of the Former Prophets, the book of Judges joins the other prophetic books in warning the people of God in every age of the deadening and deadly results of unfaithfulness. It serves, therefore, at least implicitly, as a call to repentance. Like every prophetic call to covenant loyalty and obedience, the invitation to repent in the book of Judges is grounded in the conviction that the God of Israel will be lovingly faithful to unfaithful people. Herein lay Israel's hope, and herein lies the hope of the world. Such grace is indeed free, but as the book of Judges reveals, it is not cheap. It demanded of Israel, and it demands of us, our souls, our lives, our all—in short, it demands that we worship and serve God alone.

In a world full of idolatrous and deadly distractions, in a liminal age in which God's creational purposes seem threatened on an unprecedented scale, in a social milieu that encourages and rewards excessive individualism and self-assertion, the perennial theological issue that begins and pervades the book of Judges may be especially urgent: Will we worship and serve God alone?

25

PART ONE

From Joshua
to the Judges

Judges 1:1—3:6

The story of the first judge, Othniel, does not begin until 3:7. Therefore 1:1—3:6 is usually considered to be the prologue to the book of Judges, providing a sort of double introduction (1:1—2:5 and 2:6—3:6). Both introductions begin by mentioning Joshua; but, chronologically speaking, they seem to be out of sequence. The death of Joshua is mentioned in 1:1, while 2:6 begins, "When Joshua dismissed the people . . . ." The two introductions may derive from different editors, although both seem to be dependent on the book of Joshua. While their perspectives do differ, the two introductions may be heard as parallel and complementary. Judges 1:1—2:5 introduces the book from Israel's perspective; and 2:6—3:6 introduces the book from God's perspective (Klein, 13). Or, in slightly different terms, 1:1—2:5 deals with military failure; and 2:6—3:6 deals with religious failure (see Younger, 222–23). But, from the perspective of the book of Judges, these two realms—the military and the religious—are finally inseparable. Thus, the two introductions should be heard together as a single prologue. Both serve to alert the reader to attend to the progressive deterioration that characterizes the entire book of Judges.

1:1—2:5
Fighting and Smiting: The Canaanites Remain

Scholars have long concluded that Judges 1:1—2:5 gives a different view of the possession of the land than the one found in the book of Joshua. The book of Judges, it is maintained, frankly acknowledges that Israel did not drive out the Canaanites (1:29; see also 1:19, 21, 27, 28, 30, 31, 32, 33; 2:3). In this sense, scholars have pointed out, the

27

account in Judges 1:1—2:5 is more historically accurate than the book of Joshua, because it allows more clearly for the complexity of Israel's settlement in Canaan. But this should not be taken to mean that this passage is anything like a modern historiographical account. Like the book of Joshua (and like the second introduction in Judg. 2:6—3:6), Judges 1:1—2:5 is highly stylized. In fact, the book of Joshua itself has already admitted that the Israelite tribes had not really driven out all the inhabitants of the land; and the account in Judges 1:1—2:5 actually parallels portions of the book of Joshua (especially material in Josh. 15—19; compare Judg. 1:11–15 with Josh. 15:16–19; Judg. 1:21 with Josh. 15:63; Judg. 1:27–28 with Josh. 17:12–13; Judg. 1:29 with Josh. 16:10).

The differences between Joshua 1—12 and Judges 1:1—2:5 (and, indeed, the differing perspectives within the book of Joshua itself) may be important to historians, but they are also important for those who seek to interpret the books of Joshua and Judges theologically. The built-in contradictions and discrepancies are an invitation for readers not to interpret the narratives literally. Rather, the shape of the text itself deflects attention away from matters of historicity, and it thus invites a theological interpretation.

How, then, has the material in 1:1—2:5 been stylized; and what theological dimensions are thereby suggested? This passage is held together by repeated occurrences of the Hebrew root 'ālâ, "go up," in 1:1, 2, 22; and 2:1. The first occurrence of the root introduces the primary issue involved in 1:1—2:5. The second occurrence of 'ālâ introduces a section (1:2–21) that begins to answer the question posed in 1:1. Judah goes up first, is allotted the most material, and largely succeeds, although not completely (see 1:19, 21). The third occurrence of 'ālâ introduces a section devoted to the house of Joseph (1:22–36). While there is some initial success in vv. 22–26, the rest of chapter 1 is dominated by the repeated observation that particular tribes "did not drive out the Canaanites" or the inhabitants of particular cities (1:27, 28, 29, 30, 31, 32, 33). This increasing failure becomes the subject of the section introduced by the fourth occurrence of 'ālâ. The northern tribes—although apparently strong enough to subject the Canaanites to "forced labor" (see 1:28, 30, 33, 35)—did not drive out the Canaanites or devote them to destruction in accordance with Deut. 20:16–18 (see Judg. 1:8, 17). Therefore the LORD "will not drive them out" either (2:3). In short, there will be negative consequences for the Israelites' failure to obey God.

That the issue is ultimately the obedience that derives from covenant loyalty, not simply the fighting (see the root lḥm in 1:1, 3, 5,

28

8, 9) and smiting of Canaanites (see the root *nkh* in 1:4, 5, 10, 12, 13; NRSV "defeat[s]") is suggested by the obvious priority of Judah in 1:1—2:5 as well as the attention directed to Jerusalem (1:7, 8, 21). To be sure, the attention to Judah and Jerusalem may reflect the historical ascendancy of the Davidic monarchy and the survival of the southern kingdom beyond that of the northern kingdom; but the monarchy was entrusted precisely with the establishment of God's will. And, as the larger prophetic canon recognizes, when the monarchy failed to do God's will, it and Jerusalem were destroyed (see Introduction, section 3). But as the larger prophetic canon also affirms, Jerusalem will be the site of God's eventual establishment of justice for all nations (Isa. 2:1–4). The focus on Judah and Jerusalem invites attention to the larger context of the prophetic canon. The humbling of Adoni-bezek, for instance, happens in Jerusalem (1:7). The later humbling of the Judean monarchy will also happen in Jerusalem, suggesting ultimately that God plays no favorites. God wills justice and righteousness, and the failure to embody it will eventually bring any people down.

This perspective also means that the Canaanites in 1:1—2:5 must be understood not simply as foreigners whom God hates. Rather, they should be understood to symbolize an oppressive, unjust system (see Introduction, section 3b). From this perspective, the subjection of the Canaanites "to forced labor" in chapter 1 is *not* a good thing. Rather, it represents Israel's collaboration with, rather than their demolishment of, an oppressive system. Thus, this is not a mark of success but of failure. What the Canaanites represent—an oppressive, death-dealing system—must be wiped out. In short, despite its repeated promises at the end of the book of Joshua to serve God faithfully (see Josh. 24:18, 21, 24), Israel disobeys God.

Thus, the stylization of chapter 1 that gives priority to Judah also communicates a progressive failure on the part of the Israelites. Even Judah's initial successes give way to failure (1:19–21), and the brief initial success of the house of Joseph is heavily outweighed by its series of failures. This pattern of progressive failure is a fitting introduction to the book of Judges, because it anticipates the rest of the book in two ways. First, chapter 1 moves geographically from south to north by way of its sequence of Judah/Simeon, Benjamin, Joseph, Manasseh, Ephraim, Zebulun, Asher, Naphtali, and Dan. The series of judges, beginning in 3:7–11, is not identical geographically; but it also moves from south to north: Othniel (Judah; see 1:11–15), Ehud (Benjamin), Deborah (Ephraim), Gideon (Manasseh), Tola (Issachar), Jair (Gilead), Jephthah (Gilead), Ibzan (Judah), Elon (Zebulun), Abdon (Ephraim), Samson (Dan, which eventually was located in the north). Second, and

more important, the increasing failure evident in chapter one anticipates the progressive deterioration that occurs throughout the rest of
the book (see Introduction, section 2c). While Othniel and Deborah are
relatively successful, the subsequent judges are increasingly problematic; and the book of Judges ends in utter chaos in chapters 17—21.

Not surprisingly, the end of the book will explicitly recall chapter
1. The book ends, as it began, with fighting and smiting; but in the end
(chaps. 20—21), the Israelites are fighting *each other.* The question and
answer in 20:18 especially recalls 1:1: "Judah shall go up first" (20:18),
but Judah will be fighting Benjamin! Perhaps, this is no surprise, since
"In those days there was no king in Israel; all the people did what was
right in their own eyes" (21:25; see 17:6; 18:1; 19:1). But, as Judges 1
makes clear, "the moral or spiritual decline is evident from the very
beginning of the book of Judges" (Younger, 217). And what's more, the
problem is the same throughout the book. The repeated formula in
chapters 17—21 clearly identifies Israel's self-centeredness and self-
assertion as the problem. But, as Klein points out, this same problem is
at the heart of 1:1—2:5. While Judah does go up first, Judah immediately draws Simeon into the picture. And as the chapter unfolds, the
other tribes fail to drive out the Canaanites, even when they are operating from a position of strength. Klein concludes:

> Thus, from the outset, Israel exerts self-determination, evidencing
> automatic trust in *human* perception. These verses [1:1–3] may be
> regarded as introducing the ironic configuration of the book—
> implicit difference in perception between Yahweh and Israel and
> Israel's insistence on following human perception. (Klein, 23)

In short, from beginning to end, the book of Judges is about self-
assertion and idolatry, the refusal to acknowledge and respond to God's
sovereign claim. The progressive deterioration that characterizes 1:1—
2:5 and the entire book of Judges communicates the disastrous consequences of Israel's failure to worship and serve God alone. In this sense,
the book of Judges is, like all the prophetic books, a call to covenant loyalty—a call to turn away from self-assertion and to worship, serve, and
obey God alone.

Judges 2:1–5 names and explicitly describes the disobedient self-
assertion that has been implied in chapter 1. The Israelites "have not
obeyed" God's "command" (2:2). The fact that this message is delivered
by "the angel of the LORD" (2:1, 4), as well as the content of the message, recalls Exod 23:20–33, where Israel is told not to make a covenant
with the Canaanites (Exod. 23:32; cf. Judg. 2:2) and is warned that the
presence of Canaanites and their gods will prove to be "a snare to you"

(Exod. 23:33; cf. Judg. 2:3). As suggested in the Introduction, the Canaanite system symbolizes oppression and inherently invites idolatry, and any remnant of it in the land will mean that God's will is compromised. Israel's God will not be properly worshiped in the presence of other gods, and God's purposes will not be realized. The rest of the book of Judges will demonstrate this. It will reveal a God who "will never break my covenant with you" (2:1), but whose will can be and is continually thwarted by the people's disobedience. Judges 1 has already shown the Israelites "what you have done" (2:2); and it will be what they continue to do throughout the book of Judges—that is, thwart God's will by their persistent disobedience and self-assertion. While God upholds the covenant (2:1), the people clearly do not.

As suggested above in this section and in the Introduction (sections 3a and 3b), it is crucial that the obliteration of the Canaanites and their system be heard symbolically. To devote them and their system to destruction (see 1:17) does not mean that God hates non-Israelites, but rather that God opposes idolatry and oppression. The Canaanite system represents forces that yield death, so its presence in the land is as intolerable as Pharaoh's death-dealing policies were in the land of Egypt. To oppose the Canaanite system is, in essence, to choose life as God intends it. But it is precisely this choice that the people have *not* made in chapter 1, and will not make throughout the book of Judges. Quite appropriately, therefore, the events in 2:1–5 unfold at a place called Bochim, "Weeping (Ones)" (2:5).

As it turns out, the name "Weeping" is another way in which 1:1—2:5 anticipates the rest of the book. Just as 1:1 is echoed in chapter 20, so are 2:1 and 2:5. That is to say, the people are still weeping at the end of the book of Judges. If anything, the events narrated in chapter 20 are even more tragic than the future anticipated in 2:1–5. Not only do the Canaanites and their gods become "a snare" to the Israelites, but also the Israelites become "a snare" to themselves! There is weeping in 20:23, 26 because Israelites are being killed by their own kinfolk, and there is weeping in 21:2 because the people realize that their bloody civil war has virtually wiped out the tribe of Benjamin. As Martin Tate suggests, "Perhaps we could call the book of Judges a book of weeping" (Tate, 34). Ultimately, what the people are weeping about is the reality that they and their leaders—the judges or "bringers of justice" (see Introduction, section 2a)—have failed miserably to serve and obey God alone. The consequences are disastrous. Thus, the weeping of the people at the beginning and end of the book communicates in yet another way the progressive deterioration that characterizes the entire book of Judges.

31

The other extended narrative in 1:1—2:5 is 1:11–15, and it too provides several hints of things to come, including the progressive deterioration. At first sight, this story appears to deal with what the whole book of Judges will be about—Israel opposing its foreign oppressors. A closer look proves to complicate things considerably. For one thing, while 1:11–15 (and the nearly identical story in Josh. 15:16–19) clearly associates Caleb with the tribe of Judah (see also Num. 13:6), it is possible to construe 1:13 to mean that Caleb and Othniel are Kenizzites, who are elsewhere described as descendants of Edom (Gen. 36:11, 15, 42) and among the people to be displaced when Israel occupies the land (Gen. 15:19). As Danna Fewell frames the issue: "Here is the question: Are Caleb, Achsah, and Othniel Israelites, or are they foreigners?" (Fewell, "Deconstructive Criticism," 139).

This question is not easily answered; but the very *uncertainty* surrounding this question is instructive. To be sure, this uncertainty may be approached in terms of the historical complexity of who constituted Israel and of how Israel took possession of Canaan, which very probably involved a process in which Israelites entering Canaan from outside were joined by disaffected and dispossessed peoples within Canaan to oppose the oppressive Canaanite city-state system (see Exod. 12:38, 49, which indicates this complexity). But more is at stake than the reconstruction of history. In terms of the book of Judges itself, this uncertainty reinforces the conclusion that was reached above on canonical grounds—namely, that the book of Judges cannot properly be interpreted to mean that God simply favors Israelites at the expense of other peoples. Or again, the Canaanites in the book of Judges must not be understood simply as a group of foreigners but rather as symbolic of an idolatrous and oppressive system that God opposes.

Another aspect of 1:11–15 that anticipates the rest of the book of Judges is the prominence of the female character Achsah. To be sure, on the one hand, Caleb's offer of Achsah as a prize for the most macho male military hero seems thoroughly patriarchal. If so, however, Achsah proves to have a mind and will of her own; she is not just the trinket that her name might suggest ("Achsah" seems to mean an ornamental anklet or bangle). Rather, she demands "a blessing" (1:15; NRSV "present"), and she gets it! (See Matthews, "Female Voices," 9).

While such assertiveness may reflect the conditions of a more egalitarian society that existed in premonarchic Israel (see Introduction, sections 2b and 3d), the prominence of Achsah also clearly anticipates the major roles that women will play throughout the book of Judges. Like Achsah, several women are portrayed as active and assertive in the public sphere, especially Deborah and Jael (chaps. 4—5). But, as the

32

book of Judges proceeds, the portrayal of women changes considerably. They become not leaders like Achsah, Deborah, and Jael, but rather the victims of abuse. In this regard, it may not be merely coincidental that Achsah is riding on a donkey (although the Hebrew verb that NRSV translates as "dismounted" is subject to other understandings). The next time a woman is riding on a donkey is in Judges 19:28; and the woman, the Levite's concubine, is a corpse, having been brutally abused, raped, and killed. Thus, by way of the contrast between Achsah and the Levite's concubine, 1:11–15 is yet another way that 1:1—2:5 anticipates the progressive deterioration that characterizes the book of Judges.

What is the teacher and preacher to do with Judges 1:1—2:5, a text so obviously full of fighting and smiting? A first step might be to use the text itself as an explicit invitation to readers and listeners to reflect upon the nature of Scripture. This move would be especially appropriate in an introductory session of a series devoted to the book of Judges. What many people in the church need to learn, and appreciate learning, is that the Bible itself encourages readers not to interpret it literally. In this case, the obvious discrepancies between Judges 1:1—2:5 and Joshua 1—12 (as well as the varying perspectives within the books of Joshua and Judges themselves) virtually demand that the material be approached theologically. As A. Katherine Grieb puts it, Scripture contains within itself its own hermeneutic of suspicion. "It is evident that throughout the range of biblical texts, Scripture itself does teach a hermeneutics of suspicion towards Scripture which, far from being the opposite of faithful reading, is instead an essential component of faithful reading" (Grieb, "Feminist or Faithful"). In other words, the task of the faithful interpreter is to take Scripture seriously rather than literally.

To take Judges 1:1—2:5 seriously rather than literally will mean to discern what theological function is served by all the fighting and smiting and to reflect carefully on what the Canaanites symbolize. Because the Canaanites in the book of Judges symbolize an oppressive, unjust system (see Introduction, section 3b), opposition to the Canaanites means openness to God and God's way—in short, covenant loyalty. As suggested by Klein, the real problem in Judges 1:1—2:5 is the Israelites' failure to attend to God's will and their choice to assert themselves. If human self-assertion is indeed the issue, then Judges 1:1—2:5 could hardly be more relevant in a contemporary setting. Novelist Walker Percy called the twentieth century "the Century of the Self" (Percy, 12), and the opening of the twenty-first century looks no different. In fact, from Genesis 3 onward—including Judges 1:1—2:5 and the whole book of Judges—the Bible is the story of humanity's choice to assert itself

33

instead of submitting to God. So, while what we face today is not new, it may be particularly problematic in a setting where the focus is ever more sharply on the human self and its capabilities.

As Genesis 3 suggests in moving to Genesis 4, human self-assertion results in violence. The stylized structure and movement of 1:1—2:5, as well as the links between this passage and the end of the book of Judges, suggest the progressive deterioration that characterizes the whole book. In short, the book of Judges makes it increasingly clear that human self-assertion—in the form of Israel's idolatry and disobedience—produces chaos and violence. The book of Judges, like all the prophetic books, is finally an invitation to covenant loyalty, which means to repent of self-assertion, to submit to God's way, and to experience the peace that results from the embodiment of what God wills for all the world. From this perspective, the fighting and smiting in 1:1—2:5 can ultimately be heard not as a message about the barbaric conditions of ancient peoples and places, but rather as a message about our own horribly violent North American society. The book of Judges may be a violent book, but its ultimate purpose is to communicate the disastrous consequences—including violence—of failing to attend to God and God's will. By its very foregrounding of violence, the book of Judges may be capable of being the mirror in which we see our own violent lives and times. If so, it may then even help the church find its voice to oppose the idolatries and injustices among us that continue to result in violence.

As 2:1–5 makes explicit, the self-assertion communicated in chapter 1 is finally a matter of idolatry. If we don't worship God, then in one way or another we'll end up worshiping ourselves and our own "creations." This truth will become even clearer in 2:6—3:6, the second of the introductions that comprise the prologue to the book of Judges.

2:6—3:6
Serving God or Serving Baal?

Like 1:1—2:5, the second introduction to the book of Judges begins with a reference to Joshua, although in 2:6 Joshua is alive again (cf. 1:1). Also like the first introduction, 2:6—3:6 is based in part on the book of Joshua. In fact, 2:6 recalls Joshua 24:28; 2:7 recalls Joshua 24:31; and 2:8–9 recalls Joshua 24:29–30. In other words, Judges 2:6–9 picks up the narrative sequence from the concluding chapter of the

book of Joshua, as if Judges 1:1—2:5 has been something of an inter-
ruption. Even so, as suggested above, it is helpful in the final form of
the book of Judges to consider 1:1—2:5 and 2:6—3:6 as parallel and
complementary. In particular, 2:6—3:6 explicitly suggests that the
Israelites' self-assertion in 1:1—2:5 is ultimately a matter of idolatry and
that the effects will be increasingly problematic.

The issue in 2:6—3:6, as in Joshua 24, is which deity Israel will
serve—the gods of the new land or the LORD (see Josh. 24:14–27). The
centrality of this issue is signaled by the occurrence of the Hebrew verb
ābad, "serve" (NRSV "worship") in 2:7 and 3:6, forming an envelope-
structure for this second introduction. Also, the verb is repeated in 2:11,
13, 19. Only in 2:7 is the LORD the object of the people's worship. In
each of the other instances, the people are worshiping/serving Baal, the
Astartes, and/or the gods of the land. Thus, the pattern of usage of the
verb *ābad* articulates the progressive deterioration of conditions that
has already been suggested in 1:1—2:5 and that will characterize the
entire book of Judges (see Introduction, section 2c).

What distinguishes 2:6—3:6 from 1:1—2:5 is the introduction of
the pattern that will recur in chapters 3—16. It begins in 2:11, and not
surprisingly the Israelites' "evil" is defined in terms of whom they worship or serve—the Baals. The Hebrew word *ba'al* means "lord, master."
Thus, the problem is that the Israelites are failing to set God above all
others, a violation of the Ten Commandments (see Exod. 20:1–3) and
the covenant made at Sinai (see Exod. 24:1–11), and a violation of the
covenant that has been remade in Joshua 24:14–27 (note the repetition
of the verb *ābad* in Josh. 24:14, 15, 16, 20, 21, 22, 24, as well as the
explicit mention of covenant in v. 25, anticipating Judg. 2:20). The
description of the first element of the pattern—Israel's "evil"—
concludes in 2:13; and again, it is noted by repetition of the verb *ābad*
that Israel "worshiped Baal and the Astartes [the female consort of
Baal]." Thus, repetition of *ābad* forms an inclusio for 2:11–13, just as it
forms an inclusio for the larger unit, 2:6—3:6. Again, the issue is whom
the Israelites will serve/worship.

The second element of the pattern is found in 2:14–15, and it
involves God's "anger," which motivates God to hand the people over
to their "enemies." It sounds as if this second element of the pattern
affirms simply that God punishes the wicked Israelites. And, it would
seem, if the book of Judges involves the bringing of justice, then God's
justice is retributive or distributive—God rewards good people and
punishes bad people. But, a closer look reveals that the moral equation
is *not* this simple. For instance, the same Hebrew word designates the
"evil" (v. 11) that the Israelites did and the "misfortune" (v. 15) that God

35

brings. This suggests the interesting possibility that what appears to be divine punishment in an active sense is actually the people's experience of the destructive effects of their own selfish choices (see 1 Sam. 8:1–18, where the issue is justice and where the people finally will experience the destructive consequences caused by the king "whom *you have chosen for yourselves*," according to v. 18; emphasis added). In short, God is portrayed not as a vengeful God who must act to punish, but rather as a loving God who respects the integrity and freedom of the covenant partners (see 2:20), even when these partners make idolatrous choices that produce injustice and destructive consequences like "great distress" (Judg. 2:15).

This conclusion is reinforced by the third element of the pattern that is introduced in 2:16. God's activity in the situation involves the raising up of "judges," or, as suggested in the Introduction, "bringers of justice." What the judges effect is *not* punishment, but rather *deliverance* (2:16, 18), the Hebrew of which can be and often is translated as "saved" or "salvation." Notice carefully the dynamic involved here, especially when it is put in explicitly theological terms. God's covenant partners, who have "abandoned the LORD" (2:12, 13) and "worshiped [or "served"] the Baals" (2:11; see 2:13), are delivered anyway! What this would be called, in theological terms, is salvation by grace! Thus, one cannot simply conclude that a mechanistic, retributional scheme is at work here. If the pattern is Deuteronomistic, as is usually asserted (probably correctly), then it is crucial to notice that the Deuteronomistic formulation itself undercuts any consistent doctrine of retribution. Ultimately, God's attempts to set things right will not take the form of distributive or retributive justice, but rather a righteousness that will be achieved only by God's grace (see Introduction, sections 2c and 4).

The fourth element of the pattern—the death of the judge and the relapse of the people into idolatry and disobedience (2:19)—reinforces again that God finally pursues justice in the book of Judges by way of grace. As the main body of the book of Judges will show, the pattern is repeated several times. To be sure, the people experience the negative consequences of their self-assertion, idolatry, and disobedience, but God *repeatedly* acts to deliver them. From this perspective, grace abounds!

As suggested in the Introduction (section 2c), the recurring pattern is not repeated precisely each time. The variations, and the material associated with each judge, reveal a progressive deterioration of conditions. This aspect of the book is also anticipated in 2:19 by way of the observation that "whenever the judge died, they [the people] would relapse and behave worse than their ancestors." Thus, like 1:1—2:5, the second introduction in 2:6—3:6 suggests the progressive deterioration that will characterize the entire book.

Because the pattern laid out in 2:11–19 will serve as the organizing structural principle in 3:7—16:31, and because 2:6—3:6 focuses explicitly on the people's behavior toward God, 2:11–19 has extraordinary theological significance. Thus, it is important to consider how God is portrayed in these verses, how these verses anticipate the portrayal of God throughout the book of Judges, and how the portrayal of God in the book of Judges is congruent with God's character throughout the entire biblical canon. It is crucial to notice, for instance, that the vocabulary of 2:18–19 echoes language from two key episodes earlier in the canon—Genesis 1—9 and Exodus 32—34. For instance, the verb that NRSV translates as "behave worse" (v. 19) recalls Genesis 6:12, where it is translated "corrupt(ed)" as God observes "that the earth was corrupt; for all flesh had corrupted its ways upon the earth." The adjective "stubborn" (v. 19) occurs earlier in Exodus 32:9; 33:3, 5; and 34:9, where, as here, it describes the idolatrous behavior of the Israelites and is translated "stiff(-necked)." In both Genesis 6 and Exodus 32—34, God is grieved and angered by human unfaithfulness, God threatens to wipe out and/or abandon the people involved, and yet God finally cannot bear to be simply punitive—in short, God finally proves to be gracious, merciful, and faithfully loving (see Gen. 8:21, especially in comparison to Gen. 6:5; Exod. 34:6–10).

The same kind of God is evident in the recurring pattern outlined in Judges 2:11–19. As Judges 2:18 puts it: "for the LORD would be moved to pity by their groaning." Not coincidentally, the verb *nāḥam* (NRSV "moved to pity") also occurs in both of the key episodes mentioned above. In Genesis 6:5, 7 it has the sense of "be sorry." But Genesis 6:5–7 must be heard in light of Genesis 8:21. And when *nāḥam* occurs again in Exodus 32:12, 14, the sense of the verb is clearly different; it means "change your/his mind." *God* changes God's mind! The retributive consequences God announces are *not* carried out! The only "explanation" is that God cannot help but be gracious to a people who apparently cannot help but be unfaithful. This, indeed, is the portrayal of God throughout the biblical canon, including the prophetic books, which both demand obedience and yet promise forgiveness, and including the New Testament, where the "resolution" of God's dilemma takes the form of a cross, the ultimate act of God's grace toward an incurably sinful humankind.

But God's grace is not cheap. All along the way, the people will experience the destructive consequences of their disobedience, as already suggested by the notice in Exodus 34:7 that God "by no means

37

clear[s] the guilty." By their own choice, the people will experience crippling injustice and eventually the tragedy of exile. But all along the way, the cost of the people's unfaithfulness is also borne by God, who witnesses the people's persistent unfaithfulness and is hurt by it. But, as in Judges 2:18 (see also Judg. 10:16), God is also "moved to pity" by God's pathetic covenant partners. Thus, the recurring pattern in the book of Judges is consistent with the portrayal of God from the beginning of the biblical canon (Genesis 1—9 and Exodus 32—34), and it also anticipates the rest of the biblical story, in which God's relentless grace pursues a persistently unfaithful people—indeed, ultimately, all the way to a cross (see Introduction, section 4).

In terms of the pattern in 2:11-19, the destructive consequences of injustice, which the people choose by way of their collaboration with the Canaanite system, include oppression and persecution that the system invariably produces (see v. 18). In essence, the people's own failure to be faithful means that God will not—indeed cannot—drive the Canaanites out of the land, as suggested in 2:21 (see Webb, 121-22, 208, who suggests that the main purpose of the book is to explain why the ancestral promise of possession of the land has not been fulfilled). At this point, the second introduction to the book echoes the conclusion of 1:1—2:5, the book's first introduction (see 2:1-5, especially v. 3). But the subsequent verses, 2:22—3:6, put a different spin on this perspective; that is, two additional "explanations" are offered for the continuing presence of the Canaanites in the land. Both involve the concept of testing. First, the nations remain "to test Israel" in terms of its obedience to God (2:22; see 3:4). Second, the continuing presence of the nations is to "test all those in Israel who had no experience of any war in Canaan" (3:1).

These explanations stand in tension. It is possible, of course, to assign the explanations to various editorial stages of the book. For instance, Judges 2:21 and 3:4 recall Deuteronomy 13:1-5, where testing has to do with exclusive loyalty to God (see also Deut. 8:2, 16). Even so, the final form of 2:22—3:6 retains competing explanations side-by-side, and Wessels suggests that interpreters not miss the humor involved in describing "the Canaanites as 'sparring partners' for the Israelites to teach them war" (Wessels, 191; see Introduction, section 3e).

The suggestion is well taken. But if there is humor involved, it turns out to be ironic humor when it is heard in the context of the entire book of Judges. The Israelites do learn war! In the end, however, they use what they have learned to fight each other (chaps. 19—21)! Attention to the larger canonical context also reveals that learning war is essentially a royal function. In Psalm 18:34, for instance, it is the king who is trained for battle; and it is kings who are explicitly entrusted with carrying out God's will for justice and righteousness (see Ps. 72:1–7). The larger canonical context, including the Former Prophets, points out how the kings failed to do their job. And, in apparent recognition of this failure, the Latter Prophets suggest that God's mind about teaching war as a strategy for pursuing justice has changed. Rather, as God works to "establish justice among many peoples" (Isa. 2:4; my trans.; see Mic. 4:3), the people will *not* "learn war any more" (Isa. 2:4; Mic. 4:3; see also Isa. 7:4, where Isaiah commands King Ahaz to "be quiet" rather than prepare for war, but the king refuses to listen, justifying his action in Isa. 7:12 by saying that he "will not put the LORD to the test"). The ironic humor of Judges 3:1–2 actually anticipates this conclusion that the people will not learn war. The progressive deterioration evident in the book of Judges already shows that learning war will not contribute to the establishment of God's will. Rather, it simply produces chaos, then and now.

As for the explanation that Israel is being tested for loyalty and obedience to God, its Deuteronomistic ring clearly suggests that it was fashioned in retrospect. Even so, it is instructive, especially if the testing can be heard as something other than simply divine manipulation. For those whom God calls to be faithful in every time and place, the reality of choice and the existence of alternatives mean that life will involve a "test." In the book of Judges, Israel is called to worship/serve God alone. The alternative is the Canaanite system, symbolizing idolatry and self-assertion, and ultimately, the way of death (see Introduction, section 3b).

Then and now, the way of self-assertion seems so promising. As the book of Judges will point out by way of its recurring pattern, Israel was not able to resist, despite the efforts of the judges. As the subsequent books of Samuel and Kings will point out, the successors to the judges— the kings of Israel and Judah—were not able to resist self-assertion either. In both cases, the results were tragic. The book of Judges ends in chaos, and the monarchy led both kingdoms to destruction. The lesson? Self-assertion and idolatry produce deadly consequences. From this perspective, the book of Judges is, like all the books of the Former and Latter Prophets, a call to covenant loyalty—a call to repent of self-assertion and idolatry and a call to honor, worship, and serve God alone.

At the same time, God's involvement in the recurring pattern suggests that God's will must finally be pursued by grace. Over and over again, both in the book of Judges and throughout the Bible, God forgives the people, ultimately acting in Christ for the sake of sinful humankind. This strategy for bringing justice and *shalom* may seem too demanding for human beings in the so-called "real world"; but, on the contrary, it is our only hope. In his book *No Future without Forgiveness,* Desmond Tutu describes the miracle of a peaceful South Africa after apartheid. The miracle involved the choice not to ignore past atrocities, but rather to provide the opportunity for oppressors to publicly confess their misdeeds, to make reparations to victims, and to be forgiven without punishment. Tutu calls this process "restorative justice." Only by forgiveness, Tutu proclaims, will there be a livable future, for South Africa and for the world.

The recurring pattern in the book of Judges demonstrates that God practices "restorative justice"; for, again and again, the future of the covenant between God and God's people depends on God's forgiveness (beyond the book of Judges, see Hos. 2:16–20). By demonstrating the disastrous consequences of refusing to worship God alone and to embody God's ways, the book of Judges also invites readers in every generation to repent of idolatry and self-assertion and to submit to God. In a world like ours, a world whose future is increasingly threatened by human self-assertion and the propensity to put ourselves in the place of God, the book of Judges and its call to repent are especially timely. Given the pervasiveness of competition rather than cooperation, and given the seemingly inevitable tendency of the powerful and prosperous to conclude that they deserve the best, there is little room for optimism. But the book of Judges suggests that there is room for hope—hope in God who creates a future by forgiveness and who invites the faithful to go and do likewise.

PART TWO

The Stories of the Judges

Judges 3:7—16:31

Following the double introduction to the book in 1:1—2:5 and 2:6—3:6, Judges 3:7 initiates the portion of the book that actually features the characters generally known as the judges (see Introduction, section 2a). Beginning with Othniel (3:7–11) and continuing through Samson (chaps. 13—16), there are twelve judges (not counting Abimelech in chap. 9). This number includes the six who are usually known as major judges and whose stories are characterized by the literary pattern introduced in 2:11–19. The pattern is altered as the book unfolds, revealing a progressive deterioration in both the life of the people and the leadership of the judges (see Introduction, section 2c). Othniel, the first judge, is exemplary in every way; but Samson, the final judge within the book of Judges, errs in almost every possible way, and his death is followed by the chaotic conditions described in chapters 17—21.

3:7–11
Othniel: An Auspicious Beginning

The story of Othniel, the first judge or "bringer of justice" (see Introduction, section 2a), is very compact; and it conforms precisely to the pattern laid out in 2:11–19 (see commentary on 2:6—3:6, also Introduction, section 2c). The content of 3:7 recalls 2:11, especially the repetition of "evil" and "worshiping"/"worshiped". The description of the people's behavior as "forgetting the LORD" is unique to 3:7. Later, the people's "evil" will involve the stronger "abandoned" (see 2:12–13; 10:6, 13), and this difference may be one more subtle indication that the condition of the people grows worse and worse as the book progresses (see Introduction, section 2c). As suggested in the commentary on 2:6—3:6, where the key word is the Hebrew *'ābad* ("worship" or "serve"), the people's worshiping of the Baals and Asherahs is an act both of idolatry

41

and self-assertion—the failure to submit themselves to God and God's way.

Verse 9 is very similar to 2:14, except here the enemy is named. Scholars have proposed numerous identifications for King Cushan-rishathaim and his country (see Hab. 3:7); but there is no consensus, and such attempts actually miss the point. The king's name is clearly symbolic; it means "Cushan of the Double Wickedness," and it is almost certainly intended to be humorous (see Introduction, section 3e). The author and/or editor(s) were not interested in historicity. Rather, the humorous symbolism of the king's name and the brevity of the account of the first judge suggest that the narrative was styled to fit the larger pattern of the book. Not only do the details accord completely with the pattern introduced in 2:11–19, but also the first judge is from the tribe of Judah, in keeping with the geographical pattern contained in 1:1—2:5 (see commentary on 1:1—2:5; also Introduction, section 2c). While the tribe of Judah is not specifically named, Othniel has been associated with Judah in 1:11–15 (see also Josh. 15:15–19).

The notice that "the Israelites cried out to the LORD" (3:9) is not an explicit part of the pattern found in 2:11–19, although it may be implied there by the reference to the people's "groaning" (2:18); and it recurs in Judges 3:15; 6:6–7; 10:10. Both words recall the people's situation in Egypt where their groaning (Exod. 2:24; 6:5) and crying out (Exod. 2:23) lead to the exodus. The exodus is described as God's deliverance of the people (see Exod. 14:30, NRSV "saved"; 15:2, NRSV "salvation"), as is God's raising up of the first judge (v. 9; see also Judg. 3:15; 6:15; 10:1). In short, each episode of the cyclical pattern throughout the book of Judges should be understood as a sort of new exodus, God's gracious deliverance of the people from an oppressive, death-dealing situation. The book of Isaiah will later describe the return from exile as a new exodus experience (see Isa. 43:14–21). Thus, the Latter Prophets (the book of Isaiah) join the Former Prophets (the book of Judges) in their convergence with the Torah's portrayal (in the book of Exodus) of a God who graciously acts to deliver people from death to life. Or, in other words, the Torah, the Former Prophets, and the Latter Prophets consistently portray a God who wills and works for life within the context of the covenant that God has established (see Josh. 24:25; Judg. 2:20). To be sure, the people's disobedience has destructive consequences (3:8), but God finally acts to deliver the same people who had done "evil" (3:7). This is grace; and in both Old and New Testaments, the God of Israel and of Jesus Christ pursues God's purposes by way of grace (see Introduction, section 4).

While the mention of the "spirit of the LORD" is not part of the pat-

42

tern found in 2:11–19, it too will recur in association with later judges (see 6:34; 11:29; 13:25; 14:6, 19; 15:14). But when it recurs, the contexts indicate that its effects grow increasingly problematic. Here the spirit leads immediately to deliverance and the establishment of justice: Othniel "judged Israel" (3:10). Later, however, although Gideon receives the spirit (6:34), he devises a test that God must pass before he will proceed (6:36–40). When the spirit comes upon Jephthah, it apparently is not sufficient, so Jephthah proceeds with his tragic vow (11:29–40). As for Samson, his receipt of the spirit enables him to do impressive things, but none of them lead to the deliverance of Israel! A comparison of these contexts suggest the increasing ineffectiveness of the leadership of the judges, and thus it constitutes further evidence for the progressive deterioration that characterizes the book (see Introduction, section 2c). Only in Othniel's case does the spirit's presence lead to the immediate establishment of what God wills.

One further piece of the pattern of progressive deterioration is the report of the time that the land has "rest." Only in the cases of the earliest judges are there reports of "rest" (see 3:11, 30; 5:31; 8:28). After Gideon, whose effectiveness is already surrounded by questions, there is no more "rest." Othniel embodies the ideal, to which Ehud and Deborah measure up, which Gideon approximates, and to which the latter judges fall considerably short.

3:12–30
Ehud: "A Left-Handed Man"

If the story of Othniel in 3:7–11 is mildly humorous, by way of the name of the enemy king (Cushan-rishathiam = Cushan of the Double Wickedness), then the story of Ehud in 3:12–30 is virtually slapstick comedy. Again, the names of the characters are significant. Although it is not precisely clear what the name Ehud means, it appears to be related to the word for "one" and thus may connote something like "loner" (Hamlin, 73), perhaps calling to mind his solitary mission to King Eglon's court. The name of the enemy king of Moab, Eglon, is quite similar to Hebrew words that mean "calf" or "heifer," derived from a Hebrew root that probably means "be round." Thus, the name may mean, as Hamlin suggests, something like "little fat bull," with the probable connotation of something like the contemporary "fat cat" (Hamlin, 70; see Judg. 3:17, which observes that "Eglon was a very fat

43

man.")). So, the story of Ehud is set up as what seems like a rather lop-sided contest between Eglon—the royal "fat cat" who had been getting rich off the Israelites by raiding expeditions based in Jericho ("the city of palms," v. 13) and by collecting "tribute" for eighteen years (see 3:14–15, 17–18)—and Ehud, the "lone ranger." Of course, there is no real doubt as to the outcome. In other words, the story is a comedy in every sense of the word from the Israelite perspective: It has a happy ending, the good guys win, and it is funny.

In the terms of those who study ancient folklore, the story portrays Ehud as a "trickster." The first clue that something unusual will be happening is the way that Ehud is identified in verse 15. He is a "Benjaminite," literally, "a son of the right hand"; but, he is "a left-handed man" (literally, "restricted of his right hand"; see Judg. 20:16, where other Benjaminite men are left-handed or perhaps ambidextrous). Ehud's left-handedness apparently contributes to his ability to trick Eglon and his attendants. When Ehud entered King Eglon's presence, he probably would have been searched; but Eglon's attendants seemingly missed Ehud's concealed weapon because Ehud, being left-handed, would not have carried his sword on the left side of his body like most (right-handed) warriors would have (see 3:16).

Like his actions, so Ehud's words to Eglon are "tricky," or ambiguous. He first says to Eglon, "I have a secret message for you" (v. 19); but the Hebrew could also be translated, "I have a secret *thing* for you," or "I have a *word of shelter* for you." King Eglon could reasonably have expected this to be a good word or thing, especially when Ehud says further, "I have a message [word] from God for you" (v. 20). The Hebrew word translated "sculptured stones" (vv. 19, 26) normally means "idols"; and since the Moabites controlled the crossing of the Jordan near Gilgal (see v. 28), what Ehud may have seen as he crossed the Jordan were images of Chemosh, the Moabite god. Since Eglon would have known Ehud had crossed the Jordan to deliver the tribute, Eglon may even have been expecting from Ehud a favorable word from Eglon's own god, Chemosh. In any case, he is tricked. What he gets is a thing—a sword—which, in the context of the story, turns out also to be a message of judgment from Israel's God, a word that brings justice to an oppressive situation. Ehud's two-edged sword (v. 16) has anticipated Ehud's double-edged speech. Weapon and word work together to establish justice (see Ps. 149:6–9, where "the faithful" employ "two-edged swords" against the nations for the purpose of "judgment," or the establishment of justice).

Part of the bawdy humor of the story involves the details of Ehud's killing of Eglon. In fact, the story quite literally becomes bathroom

44

humor. Ehud's sword apparently pierces Eglon's bowels, so that "the dirt" (v. 22) that is released is probably excrement. In contemporary terms, figuratively and literally, Ehud beats the crap out of Eglon. When Eglon's servants return to the roof chamber, they apparently smell the odor and logically conclude that Eglon "must be relieving himself" (v. 24). They too have been tricked; and by the time they discover what has actually happened, Ehud is long gone. Against all apparent odds, the left-handed lone ranger has defeated the well-established fat cat.

In the preceding analysis, Ehud's left-handedness has been treated simply as a physical attribute; but it is likely that ancient hearers of the story would have made additional associations with left-handedness. In ancient times (and there are remnants of this today), left-handedness was considered to be inferior, unclean, and a disability. In light of these associations, Ehud's victory looks all the more impressive: The alleged inferior defeats an obvious superior; the one supposed to be unclean leaves the royal Eglon prostrate in his own dung; the apparently disabled person proves both mentally and physically more adept than his opponents.

There are perhaps other undertones to the story as well. Ehud is described as "presenting the tribute" (v. 18; see v. 17). In other contexts, this vocabulary describes the bringing of sacrificial offerings to God. Considering that Eglon's name probably means "fat bull" (see above) and that he is killed by Ehud, it seems likely that part of the ironic humor of the story is this: Eglon, the one who exacted *tribute* from Israel, ends up, in essence, being slaughtered as if he were Israel's sacrificial *offering* to God. The ironic humor communicates a sort of poetic justice. The slaughter of Eglon anticipates the slaughter of "about ten thousand of the Moabites" (v. 29), which means that the oppressor "was subdued" (v. 30).

The story of Ehud is perhaps as close as ancient Israel could come to contemporary situation comedy. Both this trickster narrative and the contemporary genre attempt to get laughs with jokes about bodily functions and ethnic humor. To be sure, Ehud's clever and courageous exploits make for a good, entertaining, funny story. But what possible theological significance might it have? Do we even want to talk about this kind of stuff in church?

To begin to get at these questions, it is crucial to realize that for a subjugated people, humor is often the only realistic means of resistance. And, in the story of Ehud, Israel is subjugated to King Eglon; they "served King Eglon of Moab eighteen years" (3:14). The verb "served" is the one that also describes the earlier plight of the people in Egypt. In Egypt, as here, the people "cried out to the LORD" (3:15); and the LORD saves/delivers. In short, the theological significance of the story of Ehud derives from the pattern into which the editors of the book of Judges have placed it—a pattern that presents each new episode as, in effect, a new exodus (see commentary on 2:6—3:6; 3:7–11; also Introduction, sections 3 and 4).

To be sure, the people's oppression is their own fault; they did "evil in the sight of the LORD" (3:12; see 2:11; 3:7). As suggested above, "evil" in the book of Judges is essentially idolatry, which amounts to self-assertion by the people; and evil always has destructive consequences. In this sense, God is "by no means clearing the guilty" (Exod. 34:7). And yet, the justice God wills and seeks is not merely retributive. In this case, and throughout the book of Judges, God ultimately shows that God is "merciful and gracious" (Exod. 34:6). For the people who have done "evil," God raises up "a deliverer" (3:15; see 2:18; 3:9) who opposes the oppressor and restores conditions that make possible life as God intends it. This is what is meant by the land's eighty years of rest (3:30; see 3:11). In short, Ehud's work brings justice; but it is justice grounded in God's grace—what was called above "restorative justice" (see commentary on 2:6—3:6), the only kind of justice that makes a future possible for sinful people, like Israel and like us.

That God uses a "trickster" like Ehud as an instrument of God's restorative justice is interesting and instructive—indeed, one might even call it *incarnational*. God uses what and who God has available, and the instruments are seldom exemplary—for instance, God used another "trickster" named Jacob, and other murderers as well, like Moses and David and Paul (see also the commentary on chaps. 13—16).

What about the violence in the story and the fate of King Eglon and the other Moabites who were killed? The Moabites in 3:12–30 are what the Canaanites and other non-Israelites symbolize in 1:1—2:5 and throughout the book of Judges—that is, a system that, like Pharaoh's Egypt, represents the way of death. Such systems institutionalize violence, and God opposes them. When Israel, God's own people, implemented such a system—that is, when the monarchy became oppressive—God opposed it too, and the result was the exile. Out of the experience of the exile, the Latter Prophets envision God's bringing of justice among all nations, a future enacted by people who will *not* "learn war any more" (Isa. 2:4). In Judges 3:12–30 and throughout the book, violence is in the service of the establishment of God's purposes. That violence is necessary is a reminder that oppression inevitably begets violence, then and now. Like all the books of the Former and Latter Prophets, the book of Judges is ultimately a call to covenant loyalty—a call to turn away from the idolatry and self-assertion that inevitably produce violence, and a call to pursue the justice for all persons that inevitably produces *shalom,* "peace" (see Introduction, sections 3b, 3c, and 4).

3:31
Shamgar: A Non-Israelite Judge?

Shamgar, the first of the so-called minor judges (see also 10:1–5; 12:8–15; and see Introduction, section 2a), gets only one verse. Since the notice of Ehud's death does not occur until 4:1, it would appear that Shamgar and Ehud overlapped. But the editors of the book of Judges were not interested in chronology or historical accuracy. If 5:6 is any indication, it would seem that Shamgar and Jael may have been contemporaries. But again, chronological consistency is not the point. Indeed, the material on the minor judges may have been inserted by the editors primarily so that the total number of judges (not counting Abimelech in chap. 9) would amount to twelve, one per tribe, although not every tribe is explicitly represented.

Indeed, in Shamgar's case it appears that he may not even have been an Israelite! No tribal identification is given, and Shamgar's name does not seem to be Israelite. Hamlin considers it to be a Hurrian name and suggests that Shamgar "was of Hurrian descent" (Hamlin, 78). The identification that does follow Shamgar's name is surprising. He is "son of Anath"; but Anath was a Canaanite goddess, a consort of Baal. So, Soggin refers to Shamgar as "a Canaanite lordling" (Soggin, 59). What is this Canaanite lordling doing in the succession of Israel's judges?

It is possible, of course, that Hamlin and Soggin are incorrect. Perhaps the association of Shamgar with Anath simply reflects the historical reality of a polytheistic context that existed in the early period when a tribal hero like Shamgar actually lived. If Hamlin and Soggin are correct about Shamgar's non-Israelite identity, however, the inclusion of Shamgar among the judges may support what many historians have suggested—namely, that Israel's "conquest" of Canaan was something of an inside job. To be sure, elements of Israel entered Canaan from the outside, with the memory of having been delivered from oppression in Egypt and with the intent of establishing a different kind of social organization. This element of Israel was then joined by disaffected and

47

dispossessed persons within Canaan—persons who were victims of the Canaanite city-state system much as the Israelites in Egypt had been victims of the Egyptian system. These Canaanites became, in effect, Israelites, as they joined forces with those who opposed the death-dealing policies of the Canaanite city-state system. If this historical reconstruction is even approximately correct, it explains how the possibly Canaanite Shamgar could become an Israelite judge. And, furthermore, this historical reconstruction reinforces the conclusion reached on canonical grounds that a major point of the book of Judges is God's opposition to deadly oppression, *not* God's favoritism to one group of people at the expense of other groups.

If the contemporary sociologists and anthropologists are correct when they tell us that human individuals and human groups tend to establish their importance only over against and at the expense of other individuals and groups (see Elizondo, 16–18), then it is critically important to realize that God wills justice for the whole world, meaning all peoples and nations. As suggested above, the explicit articulation of God's will to establish justice and peace among all nations is found in the Latter Prophets (see Isa. 2:1–4; 42:1–4), which form the larger context for hearing the book of Judges (see Introduction, section 3). Christian interpreters hear this message reinforced in the teachings of Jesus and in the apostle Paul's opening of the church to the Gentiles (that is, the nations). But in terms of Judges 3:31, it is interesting to note that this whole grand movement may be anticipated in at least some small way by the inclusion of a Canaanite lordling, Shamgar, in the succession of Israel's judges.

That Shamgar "delivered Israel" (see also 2:18; 3:9, 15; 6:15; 8:22; 10:1; 13:5) with an "oxgoad," rather than an actual weapon, anticipates the story of Samson in chapters 13—16 (see especially 15:15). Like Shamgar too, Samson will be fighting the Philistines. But, although four chapters are devoted to Samson, Samson does not accomplish in these chapters what Shamgar does in his one verse; that is, Samson does not deliver Israel. The comparison between Shamgar and Samson is revealing; it constitutes another piece of the pattern of progressive deterioration that characterizes the book of Judges. Thus the book of Judges demonstrates what is still true today: The persistent failure to serve and obey God alone will have increasingly chaotic and disastrous effects (see Introduction, section 2c).

4:1—5:31
Deborah, Barak, and Jael: Women to the Rescue

Given the unfolding sequence of judges in chapter 3, perhaps the next scene is not as unlikely as it first appears. Ehud was a clever left-handed trickster; Shamgar may not even have been an Israelite; and now, the next judge is a woman! It is Deborah, or so it seems. Clearly, Deborah plays a major role in chapters 4—5. But Barak also plays a big part, and so does Jael, who perhaps even deserves top billing (see Judg. 5:23). The "real judge" is usually considered to be Deborah (see 4:4); but perhaps Deborah, Barak, and Jael should be considered co-judges—a sort of death-defying "triumvirate" who cooperate to effect deliverance (see Introduction, section 2a). Actually, the ambiguity derives in part from the fact that the text does not explicitly say that any of the three delivered Israel (compare, for instance, 3:9, 31). As suggested below, the intent may be to emphasize the good news that God was at work through this unlikely trio—a woman named Deborah; a guy named "Lightning," who seems none too quick, brave, or brilliant; and Jael, another woman, who also seems to have been another non-Israelite, or at least married to one (see above on Shamgar, at 3:31).

Scholars have traditionally spent a great deal of time and effort arguing over the relationship of chapters 4 and 5, especially over which is the earlier text, and how and why the earlier text has been changed in the later version. The consensus is that the poem in chapter 5 is earlier, indeed among the earliest portions of the Old Testament. The difficulty of the Hebrew suggests this conclusion, as do its lyrical style and what appear to be ancient patterns of repetition (see 5:27). But, frankly, it is impossible to prove which text came first, and it doesn't really matter much anyway. The two texts obviously differ in some details and in the focus of their concern at several points (see below); however, they are more congruent and complementary than they are contradictory. In short, the canonical sequence makes good sense. Chapter 4 describes a deliverance, which chapter 5 then celebrates with some elaboration that can be attributed in part to different authorship and in part perhaps to poetic exuberance (see a similar juxtaposition of prose and poetry in Exod. 14—15).

Before looking in more detail at chapters 4 and 5, it should be noted that 4:1–7 is the only text from the book of Judges to appear in the Revised Common Lectionary. Unfortunately, the lection cuts off the story just as it is getting started. Thus, it misses the building suspense, the ambiguities, and the unexpected turns of events, including the

49

surprising ending. By leaving out all the violence of the battle (Sisera's whole army is killed by Barak and his forces!—see 4:16) and Jael's killing of Sisera, the lection seems to let the preacher or teacher off the hook; she or he will not have to talk about such brutal realities. But, of course, the preacher then may miss the startling theological claim of chapters 4 and 5: "*God* subdued King Jabin of Canaan" (4:23), and Jael is "most blessed of women" (5:24). Then too, the preacher may miss the important opportunity to talk about violence from a biblical and theological perspective with contemporary people who have recently lived through the most violent century in the history of humankind and who, if they are residents of the United States of America, currently live in one of the most violent societies in the world. To the older generation of parishioners who lived through World War II and the Holocaust (not to mention the Korean War, the Vietnam War, the Persian Gulf War, etc.), the details of Judges 4—5 should not be all that shocking. To younger parents whose children go to schools where students fairly regularly bring in guns and knives and bombs, Jael's murder of Sisera with a tent peg (probably in self-defense) should not be so surprising. And to children who have seen literally hundreds, perhaps thousands, of murders on television and at the movies and in video games, the story of Deborah, Barak, and Jael will probably seem pretty tame, maybe even lame.

4:1–24 The Prose Narrative

The beginning of chapter 4 conforms to the pattern that characterizes the book of Judges (see Introduction, section 2c). A judge dies, and the people do "evil" (4:1; see 2:11; 3:7, 12; 6:1; 10:6; 13:1). Thus, they are "sold" to an enemy (4:2; see 2:14; 3:8; 10:7), and they cry out to God for help (4:3; see 3:9, 15; 6:6). In this case, the enemy is "King Jabin of Canaan." Joshua is said to have defeated a King Jabin of Hazor (Josh. 11:1–5); but the details of the account of Joshua's victory differ from Judges 4, so the relationship between the two is unclear. In any case, King Jabin plays very little role in the story, disappearing until 4:23–24. Sisera is really the main Canaanite opponent (see Ps. 83:9). Perhaps the author/editors of the book of Judges borrowed the name "Jabin" from Joshua 11, or perhaps "Jabin" was a throne name and there were several kings with this name. The name means "he will understand"; and in the context of Joshua and Judges, it has a sarcastic ring; that is, the king "will understand" that the God of Israel opposes oppressors.

The pattern found in Judges has theological significance (see Introduction, section 4, as well as the commentary on 2:6—3:6). To be sure, it suggests that there are consequences for disobedience, which always has negative results. But the pattern also affirms that God hears the cries of those who have disobeyed. In short, God ultimately pursues justice by grace. So, each new deliverance throughout the book of Judges is, in effect, a new exodus. In this case, it is not surprising to read that Sisera "had oppressed" the Israelites (4:3). Oppression is precisely what the Israelites had experienced in Egypt, where they cried to God for help (Exod. 3:9). The mention of Sisera's chariots also recalls Pharaoh's chariots (Exod. 14:23–28); and the description of the deliverance, especially in the poem in chapter 5, recalls the exodus account.

Actually, the pattern in chapter 4 is not quite typical; the final piece is missing. At the point where we expect the news that God "raised up" (see 2:16; 3:9, 15) someone to be a judge, we get the beginning of the story of Deborah (4:4). To be sure, we are told that she "was judging Israel" and that "the Israelites came to her for judgment [or: justice]." In this regard, Deborah seems to be the only judge who clearly functioned in a legal capacity (until Samuel, whose story lies beyond the book of Judges). But if Deborah is unique, she is not entirely so. Although it is not explicitly stated that Deborah delivered Israel, she clearly played a major role by way of her interaction with Barak.

So, even if judges are understood primarily to be deliverers rather than legal functionaries, Deborah still must be understood as a judge, or at least a co-judge with Barak and Jael. There has been an active scholarly debate about the precise role of Deborah; but the significance of this debate is minimized if judges are viewed in the broadest sense as "bringers of justice" (see Introduction, section 2a). Along with Barak and Jael, Deborah participates in bringing what God intends—that is, deliverance from oppression, or in a word, justice.

But if Deborah is a judge, she is also clearly more than a judge. She is also "a prophetess" (4:4); and, of course, the prophetic role regularly aims at justice as well (see Amos 5:21–24; Isa. 1:17; Jer. 21:12; Ezek. 34:16). The name "Deborah" appears to mean "bee," but it contains the same consonants as the Hebrew root for "speak" and "word." It is at least possible that Deborah's name suggests the prophetic role of speaking God's word. Deborah's role in delivering Israel is played out primarily by her speaking to Barak; the actual "sting" is delivered not by Deborah but rather by Barak, and especially by Jael.

Deborah is further identified by a phrase that NRSV translates as "wife of Lappidoth" (v. 4). This may be correct; but the phrase can also be translated "woman of torches." And in the context of the story, this designation makes a lot of sense. We hear nothing of Lappidoth, if this is indeed the name of Deborah's husband. And the designation of

51

Deborah as "Torch Lady" would be quite appropriate. While ancient Hebrew may not have had our English idiom "to carry the torch," there are passages in the Old Testament in which torches signify conquering power (Zech. 12:6; Dan. 10:6; see Isa. 62:1); and Deborah embodies such power (see Judg. 5:7). Furthermore, the Hebrew word usually translated "torch" sometimes describes "lightning." This is interesting, because the name "Barak" means "Lightning." While possibly coincidental, the association may suggest what appears to be the case in the story; that is, Barak cannot shine without Deborah. Or, to put it slightly differently, it is Deborah who lights a fire under Barak, who cannot, or at least will not, go into battle without Deborah (4:8–9).

This aspect of the story emphasizes Deborah's prophetic role as well. Not only does Deborah tell Barak what God "commands" him to do (4:6–7), but also Barak treats Deborah as other Israelite combatants elsewhere treat the ark, the symbol of God's presence and power. That is to say, it/she must accompany the armies into battle (see 1 Sam 4:1–3)! From this perspective, it seems that not only does Deborah speak for God; she also somehow embodies God's presence, at least in Barak's opinion.

Granted, Barak's role in the story is surrounded by ambiguity. Does his reply to Deborah in verse 8 suggest that he does not trust the divine word she has delivered? Or is Barak scared? Or does he have such a high opinion of Deborah as an embodiment of God's presence and power that he does not dare to go into battle without her? We cannot be sure, but there is nothing in the story that precludes the latter possibility. And nothing further in the story indicates that Barak was untrusting or scared. When Deborah says, "Up! [i.e., Go!]," Barak responds immediately and quite effectively. Although Deborah has suggested that Barak's pursuits "will not lead to your glory" (v. 9), Barak doesn't do too badly. He and his warriors rout the army of Sisera; and, except for Sisera, "no one was left" (v. 16). Not a bad day's work! Barak should not be embarrassed, and apparently he is not. He sings with Deborah, according to 5:1, and his contribution is appropriately celebrated in 5:12.

What the narrative does seem to rule out is the conclusion that commentators have sometimes reached—namely, that Deborah needed a man to do the fighting, and this is Barak's role. Although Deborah does seem to disappear from the action after verse 14, we have been told at least three times that Deborah went *with* Barak (twice in v. 9 and again in v. 10; see also v. 8). Deborah's role in the deliverance is secure; and furthermore, lest the story be used as apparent justification for separate and stereotypical roles assigned to females and males, there is still Jael's role to be reckoned with. Jael turns out to be the toughest, cleverest warrior of all! It is she who finally defeats the man who had oppressed Israel for twenty years (see v. 3).

In retrospect, the reader realizes that Deborah's words in verse 9 were anticipating Jael's role. But at that point in the story, the reader concludes that Deborah was referring to herself. All this, of course, is evidence of the effectiveness of the narrator in building suspense, employing ambiguity, and simply telling a good story. In any case, alongside the contributions of Deborah and Barak, there is Jael's culminating action. The story's building suspense obviously points to Jael's role as its most dramatic moment. In some sense, Jael is the most heroic of the three; and in complete congruence with the narrative impact of chapter 4, the poem in chapter 5 refers to Jael as "most blessed of women" (5:24).

Thus it is all the more strange and surprising that Jael has often been roundly criticized and even condemned by interpreters of the book of Judges. The indictment is that Jael violated the sacred customs of ancient Near Eastern hospitality. The apparent aside in verse 11 provides a bit of information that becomes relevant when the reader gets to verses 17–22. Although the Kenites had historic ties with the Israelites by way of Moses, Heber the Kenite had gone his own way. The name "Heber" can mean "ally," and later we learn that Heber is allied with King Jabin (or perhaps, a vassal of King Jabin), Sisera's boss and Israel's enemy. So it seems that Sisera could reasonably expect to find a friend in Jael, Heber's wife. The reader shares this expectation. But, not so!

Thus, Jael has been accused by interpreters of being treacherous, as well as inhospitable; but she has been most often condemned for the latter, probably in part because male interpreters have expected women characters to be especially hospitable. The charges against Jael need to be dropped. As suggested above, the immediate context of the book of Judges hails her as a hero (5:24–27), suggesting that Jael's work was none other than the very work of God (4:23). More to the point in terms of chapter 4, however, is that the story itself does *not* portray Jael as the primary violator of the customs of hospitality. As Victor Matthews has demonstrated, the character in the story who violates hospitality customs at every point is *Sisera!* To start with, Sisera should have gone directly to Heber, the head of the household, not to his wife's tent (4:17). Sisera's action thus insults Heber and dishonors Jael. In verse 18, Jael does seem to violate hospitality customs, since the offer of hospitality should have come from Heber. But, as Matthews points out, Sisera's *prior* violation would have put Jael on alert that something was

53

amiss. Furthermore, Sisera should not have accepted Jael's offer of hospitality. That he did so would have further indicated to Jael that something was wrong. Sisera's blunders continue. Good guests were not supposed to request things from their hosts; but Sisera makes two requests—for something to drink (v. 19) and for Jael to stand guard at the entrance to the tent (v. 20). The second request is particularly inappropriate; Sisera asks his host to lie, suggesting quite clearly that his presence is endangering the safety of his host—a major violation of the customs of hospitality. In short, quite literally, Sisera is asking for trouble.

And, of course, he gets it. Granted, Jael's actions have been misleading. Her assurance to Sisera in verse 18 is misleading; and the milk she gives him in verse 19 may have been intended to induce sleep, thus enabling her to kill him more easily. But Jael's actions, including the killing of Sisera, have been provoked by the fact that *Sisera* "had systematically violated every covenant of the code governing the actions of host and guest" (Matthews, "Hospitality and Hostility in Judges 4," 19). From the narrator's point of view, Jael's actions are completely justified. Jael is both expedient and clever, for she recognizes and removes the one who is clearly presented as a threat to her and to her household's honor. Sisera's actions, particularly his second request, give Jael every reason to believe that her life and her household are in danger. From the narrator's point of view, Jael's killing is not murder, but rather self-defense. It constitutes also, as suggested above, *God's* action (4:23). This aspect of the story invites not only an analysis of the violence from a cultural point of view, as we have been doing, but also from a theological point of view, as we shall do below.

Although such a gruesome story is not really funny, it can be considered a comedy in the classical sense—that is, it has a happy ending, at least for the oppressed and endangered. Plus, the gender aspects of the story may be intended to be somewhat humorous. For instance, the question that Sisera tells Jael to anticipate if anyone approaches her tent can be translated literally as "Is there *a man here?*" (v. 20). By telling Jael to answer "no," Sisera ironically both undermines his own masculinity and predicts his own death. Such irony is worth at least a smile (see Introduction, section 3e).

Another gender aspect of the story is more explicitly sexual. Since Sisera is a famous military commander (4:2–3), and since conquering male heroes generally had their way with women (see 5:30), and since Sisera had violated hospitality customs by entering Jael's tent, Jael may very well have feared that she was going to be raped. Instead, in what some commentators describe as a reverse rape, it is Sisera who "gets

54

nailed" by Jael—literally, by Jael's use of the hammer and tent peg, and perhaps figuratively as well, a possibility captured by the sexual connotation of the contemporary idiom used above. The sexual dimensions of the scene are even more explicit in the poem in 5:27. In any case, the unexpected poetic justice involved in this aspect of the story probably was intended by the narrator to be humorous. If not exactly intended to evoke a laugh, the narrator's "womanization" of Sisera makes the point that the story is, in the classical sense, a comedy. In other words, as Susan Niditch suggests, it presents Jael as "an archetype or symbol for the marginal's victory over the establishment . . . a powerfully charged model for all marginals, in particular women" (Niditch, "Eroticism and Death in the Tale of Jael," 52–53). Niditch's perspective begins to explain why the narrator can view Jael's violent act as the very activity of God, who regularly opposes violent oppression.

5:1–31 The Song of Deborah and Barak

As suggested above, the poem in chapter 5 is probably older than the narrative in chapter 4, and thus serves as its source. The language and style of the poem appear to be ancient; it may be "the oldest Israelite poem that has come down to us," and indeed "the earliest text in the Hebrew Bible" (Soggin, 64, 80). Furthermore, the poem seems to reflect the probable historical situation of the Israelites in the period between 1200 and 1020 B.C. In this era, the emerging Israelites would have lived in the highlands beyond and between the spheres of influence of the more powerful Canaanite city-states. Over against the Canaanite city-state system and its hierarchical organization, the Israelites represented an egalitarian alternative. Biological family and extended families would have worked together to attempt to subsist at the margins of Canaanite control. Life would have been a struggle for subsistence—a struggle to grow enough crops for food; a struggle between the agriculturally oriented Israelite peasantry and small villagers, on the one hand, and the more urbanized and commerce-oriented Canaanites, on the other; a struggle that would have required the contribution of all able-bodied persons, including women (see Introduction, section 2b and 3d).

These struggles are reflected in the poem, which assumes an oppressive situation from which the Israelites needed to be liberated. The situation is most clearly suggested in verses 6–8. Verse 6 depicts Canaanite control of roads and trade routes, apparently resulting in hardship for the Israelite "peasantry" (v. 7; see v. 11) until Deborah began to exercise leadership. The NIV of verse 7 seems closer to the

55

Hebrew text and communicates more clearly the result of Canaanite oppression:

> Village life in Israel ceased,
>   ceased until I, Deborah, arose,
>   arose a mother in Israel.

In short, Canaanite control threatened Israelite existence. Soggin translates the beginning of the Song of Deborah and Barak, in verse 2, as follows:

> Because in Israel the people have regained liberty,
> because the people offered themselves willingly,
> bless the Lord!
>
> (Soggin, 81)

The poem is, in effect, liberation theology; it describes a deadly threat, and it celebrates deliverance from it, against all odds (see v. 8, which suggests that the Israelites were virtually unarmed; see 4:3).

As verses 2 and 9 suggest, addressing the Canaanite threat requires the participation of all the people who must "offer themselves willingly." The poem thanks God for those who did "offer themselves willingly" (vv. 2, 9), commending them by tribal name (vv. 14–15b; 18). It also recognizes that some did not contribute to the effort, and it takes them to task, criticizing them by tribal or group name (vv. 15–17, 23). The lack of a unified effort also reflects the probable historical realities of the period between 1200 and 1020 B.C. There was almost certainly not an organized, centralized "tribal league." Rather, leadership was more localized and occasional. Insofar as the book of Judges gives the impression of more organized political structures, this is the result of the later editing of earlier stories and traditions, probably by the so-called Deuteronomistic Historian (see Introduction, section 2b).

The very looseness of early Israelite social and political organization, along with the requirements of a subsistence economy, probably explains why women could play such a major role in Israelite life, as they clearly do in the book of Judges, especially in chapters 4—5 (see Introduction, section 3d). The oppressive situation mentioned in 4:3 and described in 5:6–8 was reversed "because Deborah arose as a mother in Israel" (v. 7). "Mother in Israel" may be understood as a sort of office, as Dennis Olson suggests, citing 2 Sam. 20:16–19 (Olson, 787). Deborah does appear to have functioned in some sort of official legal capacity, although the final clause of 4:5 could be translated as "and the Israelites came up to her for justice." And this clause could be understood to mean that in a situation of deadly oppression, the people sought Deborah's help in effecting deliverance from death and restoration of conditions that support life as God intends it—in a word, justice. From this perspective, "mother in Israel" suggests that it was Deborah's efforts that, in effect, both gave Israel new life and nurtured the conditions that would sustain its life. In either case, the title "mother in Israel" communicates the honor and gratitude extended to Deborah by the people.

Jael, of course, is accorded similar honor and gratitude, being addressed as "most blessed of women" (v. 24). The poetic account of Jael's killing of Sisera is briefer than the narrative, the author(s) of which probably used 5:24–27 as a source. The details are congruent, except that verse 27 suggests that Sisera had been standing rather than lying down. The description of the scene is poetic, however, and it need not be taken pictorially. By having Sisera fall and saying that he "lay" at Jael's feet—more literally, "*between* her feet [or legs]"—the poet suggests the sexual dimension of the scene. The potential rapist is subdued by the potential victim; that is, the poet contributes to what is also evident in the narrative version in 4:17–22—the "womanization" of Sisera (see above).

The two key words in verse 27 are "sank" and "fell." They both occur three times, once each in each poetic half-line. The visual effect may be to reproduce the gradual motion of collapsing; but again, the poem communicates at more than a pictorial level. The Hebrew root *nāpal*, "fall," is regularly used to describe what happens to defeated warriors (see Lev. 26:8; 1 Sam. 18:25); and so the poet communicates emphatically that Jael has defeated the mighty military man, Sisera. That is to say, if Sisera's fall is literal, it is also figurative.

It is revealing that these two words, "sink" and "fall," occur together in Ps. 20:8 (NRSV "collapse and fall"), where they describe what will happen to the enemies of God's "anointed," the king. The kings, of course, were specifically entrusted with enacting and embodying justice and righteousness for the poor and needy by crushing oppressors (see Ps. 72:1–7, 12–14, especially v. 4). Thus, Jael's defeat of Sisera casts her in the royal role of establishing justice and righteousness by defeating an oppressor (see Judg. 4:3). The entire Song of Deborah and Barak is essentially a celebration of the establishment of God's justice and righteousness, as has been suggested earlier in the song by the summary of the celebration in verse 11. What is being celebrated are "the *triumphs* of the LORD" (emphasis added); but the word translated "triumphs" is more literally "righteousnesses" or "righteous acts" (NIV). In short, what Jael's activity accomplishes, along with that of Deborah and Barak, is the establishment of the justice and righteousness that God wills and that happens when oppressors are defeated.

57

That Jael, like the later monarchs, is portrayed as an embodiment of God's will for justice and righteousness explains why she is called "most blessed of women" (v. 24). This designation anticipates Elizabeth's proclamation to Mary—who has been told that she will bear a royal child ("Son of God" in Luke 1:35 is a royal title; see Ps. 2:7)— "Blessed are you among women" (Luke 1:42). Not coincidentally, Mary proceeds immediately to sing a song, the Magnificat, which, like the Song of Deborah and Barak, celebrates God's defeat of oppressors (Luke 1:51–53):

> He has shown strength with his arm;
>   he has scattered the proud in the thoughts
>   of their hearts.
> He has brought down the powerful from their
>   thrones,
>   and lifted up the lowly;
> he has filled the hungry with good things,
>   and sent the rich away empty.

The poetic account of Jael's killing of Sisera, especially by way of the repetition of the verbs "sank" and "fell" in 5:27, makes it clear that Jael "has brought down the powerful."

The power of Sisera, who is brought down by a woman, is emphasized in the lines that follow (vv. 28–30), which focus the reader's attention on another woman, Sisera's mother. At first glance, these lines may seem like Israelite gloating; while the Israelites celebrate in song, Sisera's mother is left alone, questioning the whereabouts of her son. But the answer (v. 30) that Sisera's mother provides to her own question (v. 28) reveals what is at stake throughout Judges 4—5 (and the entire book of Judges). Sisera's mother pictures her son exercising the power and might, which, to all appearances, belonged to him (see 4:3; and notice "mighty" in 5:13, 23). Before this battle, Sisera and the Canaanites had apparently been despoiling the Israelites for twenty years (4:3), so the outcome of this battle, as Sisera's mother envisions it, will only bring more of the same—further benefits for her and enhancement of her lifestyle (v. 30).

The Israelites had already been bearing the brunt of cruel oppression (4:3; see 5:6–7), and their victimization is what motivated Deborah and the Israelites to resist. Just how cruel the powerful can be is indicated by how Sisera's mother imagines the further despoiling of the Israelites by her son and his forces: "A girl or two for every man" (v. 30), or more literally, "a womb or two for every mighty man." The literal translation recalls the sexual nuances of the account of Jael killing Sisera; that is, in all likelihood for Jael and the women of the Israelites, it

58

was a matter of resistance in order not to be raped. In such situations of cruel oppression by the powerful, the powerful must somehow be brought down. The graphic way in which Sisera's mother depicts the activity of the powerful is another indication that the issue finally is the bringing of justice on God's terms, which means opposing oppressors.

As suggested above, the centrality of justice and righteousness in Judges 4—5 explains why Jael's action, along with that of Deborah and Barak, is ultimately portrayed as *God's* action. This message is clearest in 4:23, where immediately following Jael's killing of Sisera (4:17–22), the narrator announces: "So on that day *God* subdued King Jabin of Canaan before the Israelites" (emphasis added). Together Deborah, Barak, and Jael have been doing God's work. In short, the true deliverer is God, which may explain why the narrator never names any of the human characters as a deliverer. This departure from the pattern that characterizes the book of Judges (see 2:16; 3:9, 15, 31) serves to emphasize that all the action in chapter 4 has really been God's activity (see Yairah Amit, especially 101–4).

The same message is evident in chapter 5, although it is communicated differently. It is significant, first of all, that the poem begins as a song of praise to God: "[B]less the LORD!" (v. 2; see v. 9). The movement from Judges 4 to Judges 5 is the same movement as from Exodus 14 to Exodus 15—that is, an account of God's deliverance of the people from oppression is followed immediately by a song of praise to God. In both cases, what is acknowledged and celebrated is God's sovereignty. This is explicit in Exod. 15:18: "The LORD will reign forever and ever." And it is clearly implied in Judges 5:3, where "kings" and "princes" are invited to "Hear" the praises offered to God. To praise God, in essence, is to acknowledge God's sovereignty and to profess submission (see Ps. 47:5–7). Here the most powerful earthly sovereigns, "kings" and "princes," are invited to acknowledge God's sovereignty.

The function of the immediately following theophany, a description of God's appearing (vv. 4–5), is to portray God's sovereignty on a cosmic scale. Deuteronomy 33:2 also portrays God coming from Sinai and Seir. More important than the geographical references, however, is the description of what happens when God comes and goes. The whole earth and the heavens are affected, because God is a cosmic sovereign. The language in verses 4–5 is similar to that in other theophanies (such as Pss. 18:7–15; 29:3–9; 50:1–6; 68:7–8; 97:1–5; 99:1). Not surprisingly, several of these theophanies occur in psalms that explicitly celebrate God's sovereignty by affirming that God reigns or by addressing God as King (see Pss. 29:10; 68:24; 97:1; 99:1), and several of them also make it clear that the cosmic sovereign wills justice and righteousness (see

Pss. 50:4–6; 68:5–6; 97:2, 6; 99:4). In short, the theophany in Judges 5:4–5 reinforces the conclusion that God is behind all the action described in chapters 4—5, and that it all has ultimately to do with the establishment of life as God intends it.

The repeated word in Judges 5:4 is "poured." It also occurs in the theophany in Psalm 68:8; but it is particularly appropriate here, because it anticipates verses 19–21, where water plays a major role in the victory. The Wadi Kishon had been mentioned in 4:7, 13; but there is no indication in chapter 4 that its "torrent" (three times in 5:21) figured in the battle. We must remember, however, that chapter 5 is a poetic account. The point is that the cosmic elements, which are under God's sovereignty, join the battle on the side of the oppressed Israelites. Even the "stars . . . from their courses . . . fought against Sisera" (v. 20)! Obviously, the poet offers something more than a blow-by-blow account of the battle. He or she suggests that the whole cosmos is oriented to the establishment of God's sovereign will.

The cosmic dimension of the battle, including the role of water, recalls the account of the exodus (see Exod. 14:21—15:21). There too, cosmic elements are involved. God controls the waters (Exod. 14:21, 26–29; 15:4–5, 8) that sweep away the enemies, as in Judges 5:19–21. The cosmic dimension of the exodus account leads Terence Fretheim to point out that the exodus is not simply a local action against Pharaoh, but rather it involves the fulfillment of God's creational purposes (Fretheim, *Exodus*, 12–14). In this regard, it is not coincidental that the waters are driven back by "a strong east wind" (Exod. 14:21), recalling the "wind from God" that "swept over the face of the waters" in Genesis 1:2. When the wind blows back the water, there is "dry land" (Exod. 14:21), recalling the "dry land" of Genesis 1:9–10. In other words, the exodus is portrayed as a renewal of creation, an event that involves the fulfillment of God's purposes for the whole earth.

The same should be said of Judges 5:19–21 and the defeat of King Jabin and Sisera in Judges 4—5. The episode is not merely a local action against Jabin and Sisera; rather, it is part of a larger trajectory that begins with creation, includes the exodus, and later will include *God's defeat of Israel itself* when its kings turn out to be oppressors like Pharaoh, Jabin, and Sisera. The shape and movement of the book of Judges, along with the larger canonical context, reveal that God shows no partiality to Israel as such. Rather, God is partial to justice and righteousness, which means that God opposes oppressors (see Introduction, sections 3 and 4). The story contains at least one further indication of this truth—namely, that the "most blessed of women" is Jael (5:24), and she was probably not even an Israelite!

In any case, as the final verse of the poem (5:31) suggests, Jael, along with Deborah and Barak, is among God's friends. This final verse implicitly invites contemporary readers to consider how we too may join God in the divine work of crushing oppressors, God's enemies, and so take our place as well among God's friends.

6:1—8:35
Gideon and the Question of Sovereignty

The name Gideon means "Hacker," and it is derived from a verb that is used elsewhere to describe the activity of hacking down idolatrous images or shrines (see "hew[ed] down" in Deut. 7:5; 12:3; 2 Chr. 14:3; 31:1; and "broke down" in 2 Chr. 34:4, 7). Although the Hebrew verb is not used in this sense within the story of Gideon or anywhere else in the book of Judges, it apparently lies behind the name "Gideon" in order to recall and celebrate Gideon's destruction of the altar of Baal (6:25–32).

For the book of Judges and the larger Old Testament, Gideon's action in hacking down the altar of Baal is an unambiguously positive one, in keeping with the exclusive loyalty that God always wants (see Exod. 20:1–6), and in keeping with what God commanded the Israelites to do earlier in the book of Judges (2:2). Even so, it is somehow appropriate that the term "Hacker" in English is quite ambiguous. It can designate someone who does something skillfully and well, or it can refer to someone who does something carelessly and poorly. The ambiguity of the English term "Hacker" is an apt representation of the character Gideon in chapters 6—8; Gideon does some obviously good things (see 8:35), but he also does some remarkably bad things.

On the positive side, as suggested above, Gideon follows God's command to tear down the altars erected by the inhabitants of Canaan (2:2; see 6:25), and his leadership results in the defeat of the Midianites and restoration of "rest" for the land for forty years (8:28). But this is the last achievement of "rest" in the book of Judges. Conditions are noticeably worse after Gideon, beginning with Gideon's son, Abimelech (chap. 9), continuing with Jephthah (11:1—12:7) and Samson (chaps. 13—16), and culminating in total chaos in chapters 17—21 (see Introduction, section 2c). But this downward spiral has already begun in Gideon's own lifetime, despite the notice of "rest" (8:28) and alongside the "good" that Gideon "had done to Israel" (8:35). Most

61

noticeably, Gideon, who got his start by tearing down an idol's altar, reintroduces idolatry toward the conclusion of his career. The "ephod" he made becomes "a snare" (8:27), a word that also recalls chapter 2, but this time in a negative sense (see 2:3). In addition, there are more subtle signs of Gideon's growing unfaithfulness, all of which signals the progressive deterioration that characterizes the remainder of the book of Judges. These signs will be noted in the commentary below.

J. Paul Tanner has suggested that the Gideon narrative is the focal point of an elaborate chiastic structure that characterizes the book of Judges. Whether the book of Judges is actually this symmetrical is debatable; but Tanner is almost certainly correct when he concludes that "the Gideon narrative has a unique contribution to make to the theological development of the book," and that it "seems to mark a notable turning point" (Tanner, 150). As suggested above, the turning point involves the progressive deterioration that begins in Gideon's own lifetime. Contrary to the direction of his initial destruction of the altar of Baal, Gideon increasingly asserts his own will as opposed to following God's will. He ends up finally as a full-fledged idolater, and he leads the people—whom he has previously delivered—into idolatry as well! In short, the theological issue is, as it has been from the beginning of the book of Judges, sovereignty (see the Introduction and the commentary on 1:1—2:5). Will Gideon, and will Israel, recognize the priority of God's claim and the centrality of God's will? Or will they slip steadily into the twin sins of idolatry and self-assertion, which inevitably result in chaotic and destructive consequences?

While it is true that the entire book of Judges involves the issue of sovereignty, it is not surprising that the Gideon narrative—a turning point in the movement of the book, perhaps its focal point, and in any case, one of its largest blocks of material—highlights this issue. The issue is most explicit in the concluding and culminating episode in the story of Gideon (8:22–35), but it actually pervades the story, as well as the entire book.

6:1–32 The Call of Gideon and Gideon's Good Start

The story begins, as one would expect, with the rehearsal of the pattern that characterizes the book—the people's "evil" (v. 1; see 2:11; 3:7, 12; 4:1; 10:6; 13:1) and the consequent oppression by an enemy, this time the Midianites and Amalekites (see Exod. 17:8–16; Num. 31:1–12; Deut. 25:17–19). As in chapter 4, the details of the new oppression are elaborated upon, but even more extensively this time

(6:2–6). This is the first indication that things may be getting worse. Indeed, Israel "was greatly impoverished." The "impoverished" (see "weak" in Ps. 82:3, 4; "poor" in Ps. 113:7; Amos 2:7; 4:1, 8:6), however, are ones whom God looks upon favorably, especially when they cry out, as the Israelites again do here (v. 6; see 3:9, 15; 4:3). As in the previous stories in the book of Judges, God will act; and this pattern itself has remarkable theological significance. Even those who persist in doing "evil," even those who have brought oppression upon themselves, will be the beneficiaries of God's saving activity. Thus, the pattern in the book of Judges portrays a God who cannot help but be gracious. The God of the exodus continues to effect a series of new exoduses throughout the book of Judges (see Introduction, sections 3 and 4; also commentary on 2:6—3:6).

But in this case, and again like chapter 4, God does not act immediately to defeat the Midianites and the Amalekites. The pattern is modified. In chapter 4, after the Israelites cried out, Deborah was introduced; taking up her role as a prophet, she immediately proceeded to initiate activity that led to the people's deliverance. In chapter 6, after the people cry out, the modified pattern again involves the introduction of a prophet. But, in this case, the prophet proceeds not to deliver but rather to chastise the people—another subtle sign that things are getting worse.

Like the angel in 2:1–5, the prophet in 6:7–10 recalls the exodus from Egypt and the gift of land. Both of these gracious acts should have resulted in the people's giving exclusive loyalty and allegiance to God; and indeed, the book of Judges begins immediately after the people have promised three times to be faithful to the covenant (see Josh. 24:18, 21, 24). But it did not happen that way. As the angel anticipated in 2:1–5, the people have not recognized God's sovereign claim upon them. Instead, they have given their allegiance to other gods (6:10).

Another sign that things are getting worse may be the fact that now both a prophet *and* an angel are required to set in motion the process of deliverance. But even with this increased divine workforce, things will move rather slowly. Gideon will prove to be none too cooperative or faithful. Even when the "angel of the LORD" (6:11–12) becomes simply "the LORD" speaking directly to Gideon (6:14), Gideon responds with questions, excuses, and requests for proof (6:15–17).

To be sure, such behavior actually puts Gideon in some pretty good company. Indeed, beginning at 6:11, the story of Gideon is reminiscent in several ways of the stories of Jacob, Moses, and Elijah—so much so, in fact, that A. Graeme Auld has concluded that this portion of the story, at least, is a late addition to the book of Judges, written specifically to

63

recall the stories of other Old Testament worthies (Auld, 263–67). Be that as it may, "the cluster of associations with some of the most important figures of the OT raises enormous expectations about Gideon's tenure as judge and deliverer of Israel" (Olson, 797). Unfortunately, the story of Gideon will not end on nearly as high a note as it begins.

The initial greeting that the angel brings to Gideon is surprising on two counts, as Gideon's subsequent response indicates. First, it does not appear that "the LORD is with us" (6:13); and second, Gideon hardly seems like a "mighty warrior" (6:12), hiding as he is from the Midianites as he tries to eke out a daily living (6:11). Gideon's initial question of "why" (v. 13) conveniently overlooks the "evil" that the people had done (6:1). Neither the angel nor God makes any attempt to answer this question, suggesting that it is now irrelevant. The "answer" Gideon gets is a command (6:14), which, like the previous assurance of God's presence (6:12), recalls the story of Moses (see Exod. 3:10, where "come" and "send" are the same verbs that in Judg. 6:14 are translated "Go" and "commission"). In short, Gideon is being commissioned to lead a sort of new exodus.

Like Moses (Exod. 3:11), Gideon at first responds to his commission by asking another question (6:15). What Gideon does not seem to realize, but will have further opportunity to learn (see 7:2–8), is that being "weakest" and "least" is no problem with God. In fact, God prefers those so positioned—Jacob, Saul, David and, later, the Corinthians (see 1 Cor. 1:26–31)—"so that no one might boast in the presence of God" (1 Cor. 1:29; see Judg. 7:2). God's response to Gideon's objection is the same promise that God had offered in response to Moses' objection: "I will be with you" (v. 16; see Exod. 3:12).

Like Moses, Gideon will need "a sign" (v. 17). At this point, the details of the story begin to recall experiences of Jacob and anticipate those of Elijah. Fire consumes the food as it does in the story of Elijah's contest with the prophets of Baal (see 1 Kgs. 18:20–40, especially vv. 36–40); and, of course, it is not coincidental that Gideon is being called to do battle with devotees of Baal as well. Gideon's response to this event reminds one of Jacob's experience at Bethel (Gen. 28:10–22), where Jacob, like Gideon here, builds an altar—as well as of Jacob's experience at Peniel, where he saw "God face to face" (Gen. 32:30; see Judg. 6:22). At that point, Jacob became "Israel" (Gen. 32:28) and was ready to assume his divine vocation. Having met "the angel of the LORD face to face" (v. 22), Gideon is prepared as well.

Even so, and despite the divine admonition, "do not fear" (v. 23), Gideon was not exactly brave, courageous, and bold when God told him to "pull down the altar of Baal" (v. 25). In fact, he was still "afraid"

64

(v. 27), but he "did as the LORD had told him," even if it was "by night" (v. 27). Of course, the deed is soon discovered, and the people of the town are upset (vv. 28–30). Even though the altar of Baal had belonged *to Gideon's father*—another indication, perhaps, that things were getting worse among the Israelites—the father defends his son. Apparently Gideon has made at least one convert; and apparently the father's leadership convinces the townspeople not to intervene. Like Elijah, Gideon has discredited Baal and his devotees. Thus, Gideon's other name is Jerubbaal, "Let Baal contend" (v. 32), which some scholars conclude was the original name in the story (especially since the other Old Testament allusions to Judg. 6—8 refer to Jerubbaal rather than Gideon; see 1 Sam. 12:11; 2 Sam. 11:21).

So far, so good. Gideon, though remaining fearful, has obeyed God's command and has begun to restore the worship of the LORD. Destroying the altars of the gods of the land is the way that the book of Judges has stipulated for the people to demonstrate their covenant loyalty (see 2:1–3). Furthermore, Gideon "has built an altar . . . to the LORD, and called it, The LORD is peace" (v. 24). In other words, the well-being of the people and the land is coming about as Baal is opposed and the Canaanite system is dismantled (see Introduction, section 3b). Thus, Gideon is doing what the word "judge" fundamentally means. He is acting as a "bringer of justice," the result of which is always *shalom*, "peace" or "well-being" (see Introduction, sections 2a and 4). But, of course, there is still more to be done. The Midianites and Amalekites remain a threat. Gideon will succeed in defeating them; but in the process, there are several subtle signs that the good start that Gideon has made will not last. These signs suggest that, if the Gideon narrative is indeed a turning point in the book of Judges, things are turning in the wrong direction.

6:33—8:3 "For the LORD and for Gideon": The Defeat of Midian and Amalek

What seems like an unambiguously good thing—that "the spirit of the LORD took possession of Gideon" (6:34)—proves to be problematic. It may actually suggest the progressive deterioration of conditions among the Israelites and, indeed, Gideon's turn for the worse. When the "spirit of the LORD" first appears in 3:10, it possesses Othniel, the first judge; and deliverance follows immediately. Here, however, when the spirit possesses Gideon, and despite the auspicious sign that several tribes fall into place when Gideon sounds the trumpet (6:34–35), Gideon hesitates (6:36–40). Apparently, the spirit is not effective apart

65

from human participation (see commentary on 11:29–40 and 13:1–25, including the quotation from Richard G. Bowman in the latter).

Gideon needs another sign; and so he proposes another test, despite the fact that God had passed the first test with flying colors (see 6:17–24), despite the initial success against Baal and his devotees (6:25–32), and despite the most recent appearance of "the spirit of the LORD." The details of the test, which the LORD again passes with no problem, are far less important than the fact that Gideon still needed to ask for a test. As Robert G. Boling put it:

> At this point the depiction of the judges period begins to resemble the modern theater of the absurd. Gideon had exploited his sober judicial responsibility by seeking a superfluous divine "yes" or "no" before a battle. The audience of course knows, in general, that what is to follow is a sparkling account of Yahweh's victory, without Gideon or anyone else actually fighting, at first. (Boling, 141)

In short, Gideon is beginning to look at least a little ridiculous. Instead of growing more faithful, he seems to be growing more faithless and more fearful. Indeed, this situation suggests that the place names in 7:1 have more than geographical significance. Gideon and his troop camp "beside the spring of Harod," a name that is nearly identical to the word translated "trembling" in verse 3. The enemy is near "the hill of Moreh," or "Teacher's Hill," perhaps anticipating that the turning point in the attack comes when Gideon is instructed by a Midianite soldier interpreting a dream for his comrade (7:13–15).

Before the attack, Gideon's forces need to be readied for battle (7:2–8). Given Gideon's previous fear (6:27) and the fact that he remains fearful (7:10), one of the most startling aspects of 7:2–8 is perhaps that Gideon himself did not return home (7:3)! The strategy for readying the troops is in accordance with Deuteronomy 20:1–8, which suggests that the army of the people of God "shall not be afraid" because "the LORD your God is with you" (v. 1). Anyone who is "afraid or disheartened . . . shall go back to his house" (v. 8). Even so, Gideon stays, as do ten thousand more. But this number is "still too many" (7:4), the danger being that the troops themselves will "take the credit" (v. 2) for deliverance away from God. As the story unfolds, this proves to be a not unfounded fear.

In any case, God prepares a further strategy for reducing the size of Gideon's army. As Soggin concludes concerning this next step, "There is considerable confusion about the character of the test" (Soggin, 137). In short, no one knows what God has in mind here. The pertinent point is that Gideon ends up with a ridiculously small fighting force—300 men to go up against the forces of the Midianites and Amalekites that number over 135,000 (see 8:10). This definitely should ensure that there will be no danger of taking the credit away from God. After all, this is the theological point of this obviously hyperbolic and stylized account and of the entire "holy war" provisions—to affirm that any and every victory is a gift of God.

Despite the "holy war" guidelines in Deuteronomy 20:1–8, and despite the divine promise of victory in 7:9, Gideon is still afraid and God knows it (7:10). So, in a display of remarkable restraint and patience, God devises yet another means to reassure Gideon (7:10–15). Gideon sneaks into the enemy camp and eavesdrops. What he hears is one soldier's weird dream and his comrade's interpretation of it, to the effect that "God has given Midian and all the army" over to Gideon (v. 14). Upon hearing this, Mr. Barley Cake (see v. 13) is ready to attack (7:15). Perhaps Gideon is encouraged by evidence of the enemy's low morale; but in any case, as Tanner concludes, "the irony is stunning: hearing the promise [of victory] directly from the Lord did not convince Gideon, but hearing it from the Midianite soldier did" (Tanner, 159).

In this view, Gideon's response in 7:15 is evidence that Gideon now has "complete confidence in God" and that he has "moved from fear to faith" (Tanner, 160). This seems like a reasonable conclusion, especially in view of the subsequent account of the actual attack (7:16–22). For instance, the bizarre military strategy that Gideon employs—torches, jars, and trumpets are the weapons—seems designed to lead the reader to conclude that only God could be responsible when such strange tactics enable three hundred men to destroy 120,000! To be sure, surprise attacks at night can be surprisingly effective; but Boling is surely correct when he concludes that the "aim of contrived unreality" suggests that this "victory was strictly analogous to the one at the Reed Sea" (Boling, 147–48). In short, as the poem in Judges 5 suggests about the victory of Deborah and Barak (see commentary on Judges 5), it is really God who has done the fighting and won the battle. In this instance, 7:22 makes it explicit that God deserves "the credit" (see 7:2) for effecting what amounts to a new exodus.

Even so, while it seems that Gideon has "moved from fear to faith," the situation may actually be more complicated. The two versions of Gideon's battle cry, "For the LORD and for Gideon!" (v. 18) and "A sword for the LORD and for Gideon!" (v. 20), suggest that Gideon may also be moving from fear to self-assertion. While from one perspective Gideon may simply be exercising strong military leadership, he also seems willing to take at least some of "the credit" (7:2) for the victory. This is not a good sign. If the primary issue in Judges 6—8 is

67

sovereignty, as suggested above, Gideon does not seem willing to see God as completely sovereign. If Judges 6—8 is a turning point, as suggested above, Gideon seems to be turning in the wrong direction. This suspicion will be confirmed in 8:4–35.

Before turning to 8:4–35, however, note that Gideon still comes off looking good in 7:24—8:3. For instance, he rallies several of the tribes to participate in the conclusion of the battle (7:23). Although the Ephraimites apparently did participate in the operation against the Midianites (7:24–25), they seem to think they have been excluded (8:1). In dealing with their complaint, Gideon proves to be an effective conflict manager, properly giving "the credit" (7:2) to God and humbly suggesting that the Ephraimites have achieved far more than he himself (8:2–3; compare the more violent conclusion of Jephthah's dealing with a similar Ephraimite complaint in 12:1–6). Thus, Gideon's behavior later in chapter 8 is all the more surprising and disconcerting.

8:4–35 Gideon's Turn for the Worse

As suggested above, Gideon's battle cry (7:18, 20) seems to indicate that his growing faith may be founded as much in himself as it is in God. Although appropriately faithful to God and humble in the presence of others in 8:1–3, Gideon proves to be alarmingly self-assertive and prideful in 8:4–21. And although he articulates the appropriate theology in 8:23, affirming God's exclusive sovereignty, his subsequent actions belie his words (vv. 24–27). As a result, the wrong turn that Gideon has taken also leads "all Israel" astray. By the end of the story of Gideon, despite the notice that "the land had rest for forty years in the days of Gideon" (v. 28), it seems that Gideon has led the Israelites back into what he had initially led them out of—idolatry, the worship of something or someone other than the LORD. This constitutes the "snare" (v. 28; see 2:3). To be sure, the Midianites and Amalekites have been disposed of; but as the conclusion of chapter 8 demonstrates, along with chapter 9, the threat from within can be just as disastrous as the threat from without.

Verse 4 confirms what the reader has suspected and what 7:23–25 has actually indicated—namely, that God did not really do all the fighting. Or, as suggested above, the "holy war" pattern is a stylized accounting that is intended to affirm that all "the credit" (7:2) for Israel's victories belongs to God alone. But, it is precisely this lesson about God's sovereign claim that Gideon appears to be forgetting in 8:4–35. Gideon supports his request for food from the people of Succoth by saying: "I am pursuing Zebah and Zalmunna, the kings of Midian" (v. 6).

68

(Emphasis has been added, but note that in the Hebrew construction, the verb is an active participle, and the first-person pronoun is present, thus lending emphasis to the "I.") Although Gideon does subsequently mention the Lord's role in the defeat of Zebah and Zalmunna (v. 7), he acts in a way that indicates that "the credit" is really his alone.

If anyone should have understood the desire of the people of Succoth and Penuel for *proof* that "the LORD has given Zebah and Zalmunna into my [Gideon's] hand" (v. 7), it should have been Gideon! After all, Gideon had previously needed repeated and rather dramatic proofs of God's saving activity (see 6:17–24, 36–40; 7:10–15). But he has no sympathy for the people of Succoth and Penuel. The humility and the conflict management skills of 8:2–3 are sorely lacking. While Gideon's killing of Zebah and Zalmunna (8:18–21) may be understood as part of the "holy war" stipulation to annihilate the enemy (see Deut. 20:16–18), the same cannot be said of Gideon's treatment of the people of Succoth (v. 16) and his killing of the men of Penuel. There is absolutely no indication that this behavior is divinely directed. Rather, it has every appearance of selfishly motivated personal revenge. The textual variant in v. 16 is worth noting. Although it is understandable that the NRSV has followed several manuscript traditions in reading verse 16 in accordance with verse 7, the Hebrew reading "taught" is interesting (see NRSV note). Gideon does indeed seem to be out to "teach" the people of Succoth a lesson, and the lesson seems to be something like this: "You cannot cross me and get away with it, because I am a powerful man."

Apparently, the people of Succoth are not the only ones who learned this lesson. In 8:22, the Israelites request of Gideon: "Rule over us, . . . for *you* have delivered us out of the hand of Midian" (emphasis added). Given Gideon's behavior in 8:4–21, the people's conclusion is a logical one. Gideon has done little or nothing in these verses to witness to God's sovereignty. Rather, he has been arrogant, ruthlessly self-serving, and brutally vindictive. Gideon has refused to show to others the patience that God had shown to him. It appears that Gideon has not moved from fear to faith, but rather from fear to self-assertion.

The people's request to Gideon ("Rule over us") makes explicit that the issue is sovereignty. Gideon's refusal to establish a monarchy, a dynasty, is theologically grounded, as it should have been: "the LORD will rule over you" (v. 23). Having participated like Moses in a deliverance that is analogous to the exodus, Gideon here articulates the basic theological affirmation that the exodus demonstrated: "The LORD will reign forever and ever" (Exod. 15:18). And, as Samuel suggests a bit later in the canonical sequence, the only legitimate king who rules over Israel is God (see 1 Sam. 8:1–9).

While Gideon's theological articulation is sound, his embodiment of this theology is not. In short, Gideon's actions speak far more loudly than his words. Although Olson suggests that perhaps Gideon's statement reveals that he "abandons his responsibility to lead Israel as a servant and partner with God," the problem apparently is *not* that Gideon evades the calling of leadership but rather that he exercises it poorly and unfaithfully (Olson, 809). As a judge, Gideon could rightfully claim some responsibility to lead; and, indeed, in verse 24, Gideon swings immediately into an active leadership role.

The problem, however, is that Gideon's role model at this point is no longer Moses, who, though hesitant (as Gideon had been; see above), had proven faithful and whose song affirmed God's sovereign claim (Exod. 15:1–18). Rather, Gideon's role model becomes Aaron, and indeed, Aaron at his worst moment. Gideon's first executive request clearly recalls Exod. 32:1–6, where Aaron's leadership resulted in a request for gold jewelry from which he fashioned a golden calf, which the people then treated as a god. To be sure, the details differ in Judges 8:22–28. Gideon makes "an ephod"; but the authors/editors of the book of Judges clearly suggest that, like Aaron's leadership, Gideon's leadership results in idolatry. Elsewhere, the concept of Israel prostituting itself (8:27) regularly indicates idolatry (see Exod. 34:15–16; Lev. 17:7; 20:5; Deut. 31:16; Jer. 3:1; Hos. 4:13–15); and the word is also associated with idolatry in the immediate context (see v. 33; see also "lusted after" in Judg. 2:17). Furthermore, the ephod became "a snare to Gideon" (v. 27), and "snare" was explicitly associated with idolatry in Judges 2:3.

In short, Gideon's leadership has resulted in idolatry, the very thing that Gideon had begun his career by combating when he tore down the altar of Baal. Gideon, who started out as a "hacker" in the best sense of the word, has ended up as an administrative "hacker," in the worst sense of the word. Gideon may be understood as a judge or as a would-be king (despite his denial in v. 22; note that the name of his son, Abimelech, means "my father [is] king"!). In either case, he has failed to honor God's sovereignty. In other words, Gideon has moved, not from fear to faith, but rather from fear to self-assertion and idolatry, the twin sins the book of Judges has associated with each other from the beginning (see commentary on 1:1—2:5). For this reason, Hamlin rightly calls Gideon "the flawed judge" (Hamlin, 90); and it is with Gideon that Israel's "downhill slide begins" (Olson, 791). Not surprisingly, Gideon's legacy consists of immediate idolatry by the people (v. 33; but as suggested above on the

70

basis of v. 27, this had already begun in Gideon's own lifetime and as a result of his own leadership). To be sure, this could be construed as part of the pattern that characterizes the entire book of Judges; that is, after a judge dies, the people again do "evil." But, in this case, there is a major expansion on Gideon's legacy in chapter 9. The issue is still sovereignty (see "rule" twice in 9:2), and the story will reveal the tragic and violent results of failing to worship, serve, and obey God alone.

9:1–57
Abimelech: Gideon's Violent Legacy

Judges 9 should not be sharply separated from chapters 6—8. Although Gideon has died, the events of chapter 9 are still very much a part of Gideon's story. One reason, of course, is that the major character in Judges 9, Abimelech, is Gideon's son. Furthermore, Abimelech is never identified as a judge, nor is it said that he judged or delivered Israel. He did not. Rather, he usurped power, although in a real sense Abimelech is simply following the wrong direction that Gideon himself had taken in Judges 8 (see above). After all, Abimelech's name means, "my father (is) king." To be sure, we don't know who gave him this name (maybe he adopted it for himself to further his own ambitions); but the existence of his name, along with Gideon's *deeds* in Judges 8 (as opposed to his *words* in 8:23), raise legitimate suspicions about Gideon. In any case, even if Gideon did not set himself up as some sort of king, he very explicitly denied God's sole sovereignty by reintroducing idolatry among the Israelites (8:27). Judges 9 is, in short, a portrayal of the disastrous results of Gideon's legacy.

In terms of the juxtaposition of chapters 8 and 9, it is worthy of note that chapter 8 does *not* conclude with the notice that the land "had rest" (8:28; compare 3:11, 30; 5:30), nor does it conclude with the notice of Gideon's death (8:32; compare 3:11). Rather, it concludes with a very explicit description of the people's idolatry (8:33), their failure to recognize God's sovereignty (8:34), and their neglect of what "good" Gideon had done (8:35). In short, the story of Abimelech is explicitly set in the context of the people's disobedience. That chapter 9 begins, ends, and is pervaded by violence among the Israelites themselves is a further indication that Gideon had taken a wrong turn and that things are indeed getting worse as the book of Judges unfolds (see Introduction, section 2c; also the commentary on chaps. 6—8).

71

In the final form of the book of Judges, the chaotic violence of chapter 9 and the violent chaos of chapters 17—21 form a framework or envelope around the judges succeeding Gideon. This structural feature is yet another indication of the progressive deterioration that characterizes the book. Furthermore, 12:1–6 describes the Israelite-on-Israelite violence that follows Jephthah's deliverance of the people from the Ammonite threat. This means that depictions of chaos and internal violence follow or conclude the stories of the final three major judges—Gideon, Jephthah, and Samson. Again, chapter 9 reinforces the conclusion that Gideon's story is a pivotal turning point—specifically, a turn for the worse.

The violence in chapter 9 begins almost immediately; and by virtue of the repetition of "rule" in 9:2, recalling 8:22–23, the violent actions of Abimelech are associated explicitly with the issue of sovereignty. At least Gideon had *said* the right thing about God's sole sovereignty: "the LORD will rule over you" (8:23). Abimelech, on the other hand, leaves the LORD out of the picture entirely. He simply assumes that "rule" will be either his prerogative or the prerogative of "all seventy sons of Jerubbaal" (9:2; here, as in 2 Kgs. 10:1, "sons" may designate allies or vassals of the king or ruler). Not only is Abimelech's violence linked to the issue of "rule"—the failure to recognize God's sovereign claim—but it is also overtly financed by idolatry. The money received from the temple treasury of Baal-berith is used by Abimelech to pay the thugs who help him kill the seventy sons of Gideon (9:4–5).

Again, this is Gideon's legacy. He had reintroduced idolatry among the Israelites (8:27), who immediately after (and by implication, even *before*) Gideon's death are worshiping Baal-berith (8:33). Baal-berith means literally, "Lord/Master of the Covenant," suggesting all too clearly where the Israelites are directing their loyalty and allegiance. They are no longer in covenant with God, but rather with the people and gods of Canaan (see 2:1–2). As suggested in the Introduction (section 3), the question that initiates and pervades the book of Judges is whether the people will recognize God's sole sovereignty—that is, whether they will worship, serve, and obey God alone. As in 1:1—2:5, the answer is still *no*. When God is not sovereign, someone else will be (or will attempt to be). As in 1:1—2:5, idolatry and self-assertion go hand in hand. In this case, the would-be sovereign is Abimelech. He can tolerate no competition. According to his logic, he must kill other potential sovereigns; and he does (9:5). Or he almost does; "Jotham, the youngest son of Jerubbaal" (9:5), escapes.

Jotham's "fable," as it is usually designated, is more clearly directed against Abimelech than it is against monarchy in general. On one level, the book of Judges is a setup for the Davidic monarchy; and the larger prophetic canon acknowledges a legitimate place for the institution of monarchy. From this perspective, the mistake of the people of Shechem is not so much that they made someone king, but rather that they "made Abimelech king" (9:6). Abimelech has denied God's ultimate sovereignty, and he is also clearly among those who "did not exhibit loyalty to the house of Jerubbaal (that is, Gideon) in return for all the good that he had done to Israel" (8:35).

More at issue than a particular form of government—monarchy or otherwise—is whether people relate to one another "in good faith and honor [or integrity]" (9:16). Abimelech clearly has not related to his own family with integrity. Instead, he wiped them out. Jotham's fable and subsequent address indict the people of Shechem for being complicit in Abimelech's violence. Not coincidentally, Jotham speaks from Mount Gerizim, the place that is stipulated for calling the Israelites to covenant obedience and for reminding them of the promised blessings of covenant loyalty (see Deut. 11:29; 27:12; Josh. 8:23). In the current form of the fable, which is really more of an allegory, the bramble is Abimelech. The bramble's speech (9:15) assures its own demise and the destruction of those who choose it, because a worthless bramble cannot be made king "in good faith." In terms of Abimelech, the only possible result of his being made king is disaster—for himself and for the people of Shechem. As the bramble's speech anticipates, Abimelech will eventually destroy the lords of Shechem by fire (9:46–50). In this sense, the allegory functions ultimately as "the curse of Jotham" (9:57).

Given the kind of person that Abimelech apparently was, the lords of Shechem probably would have "dealt treacherously with" him eventually, no matter what. Violent people naturally evoke violent responses. But the narrator—unlike Abimelech himself—will not leave God out of the picture; so he or she explains that unrest arose between Abimelech and the lords of Shechem because "God sent an evil spirit between Abimelech and the lords of Shechem" (9:23). This theological perspective affirms that God simply will not be content with idolatry, unbridled self-assertion, and the resulting disastrous consequences. As the entire book of Judges demonstrates, God vehemently, even violently, opposes oppressors whose idolatry and injustice threaten life as God intends it (see Introduction, sections 3c and 4).

The remainder of chapter 9 is an account of escalating violence, the logical result of idolatry and unbridled self-assertion. New characters enter the narrative—Gaal, son of Ebed, who opposes Abimelech, and Zebal, who supports Abimelech (vv. 26–41). This complicates the plot a bit; but the basic conflict is still Abimelech versus the lords of

73

Shechem, and the whole sorry episode portrays the ruthless self-centeredness and vengefulness of all parties. The reader is not surprised when Abimelech eventually captures Shechem, kills all its people, and razes the place (vv. 42–45). The principals in the conflict—the lords of Shechem—are singled out for destruction by fire (vv. 46–49). Their complicity had started the whole mess; and their destruction by fire is poetic justice, in accordance with the final lines of Jotham's poetic allegory (9:15).

For no apparent reason, other than that violence tends to become a way of life, Abimelech proceeds to attempt to do at Thebez what he had done at Shechem (9:50–55). "Abimelech's frenzied attacks of unwarranted and extreme revenge show a portrait of a madman out of control" (Olson, 817). As at Shechem, a tower is involved; and this aspect of the story also recalls 8:17, where Gideon "broke down the tower of Penuel, and killed the men of the city." This detail is yet another reminder that the events in chapter 9 constitute the violent legacy of Gideon and his turn for the worse.

The strategy that had succeeded at Shechem fails at Thebez. As Abimelech approached the tower to set it on fire, "a certain woman threw an upper millstone on Abimelech's head, and crushed his skull" (9:53). The verb "crush" is used elsewhere to designate cruel oppression (see Judg. 10:8; Amos 4:1), so it is fitting that the oppressor Abimelech gets "crushed." From one perspective, the lesson is this: those who live by the sword will die by the sword. But again, the narrator will not leave God out of the picture. From the narrator's theological perspective, "God repaid Abimelech for the crime he committed against his father in killing his seventy brothers"; and events have also served to give the people of Shechem what they deserve for their complicity with Abimelech (9:56–57; see 9:24). The demise of Abimelech and the people of Shechem demonstrate the goal of God's bringing of justice—the crushing of oppressors toward the ultimate aim of establishing *shalom*, "peace" (see Ps. 72:1–7).

Although Abimelech gets "repaid" (9:56), it is important to recall that God's justice in the book of Judges is not simply distributive or retributive. While there are inevitably negative consequences of injustice and oppression—and in this sense, God by no means clears the guilty (see Exod. 34:7)—God ultimately works in the book of Judges and throughout the Bible to pursue justice by means of grace, mercy, and forgiveness (see Exod. 34:6). Thus, although they repeatedly do "evil," the people are repeatedly delivered by God through the agency of the judges. The ultimacy of grace does *not* mean that God has no standards. The story of Abimelech illustrates powerfully what God's standards are; God wills faithfulness and integrity among humans (see 9:16), and God stands solidly against Abimelech and all other oppressors whose idolatrous self-assertion produces deadly consequences.

Since the book of Judges has often been interpreted to mean that God favors Israelites over against Canaanites and other groups of people, it is especially important to notice that Abimelech is an Israelite. This situation is another reminder that the Canaanites and other peoples in the book of Judges symbolize a particular way of life—idolatrous self-assertion that is the way of death. When the Israelites adopt this way of life/death, God opposes them too, as the story of Abimelech shows, as does the later demise of the monarchy when it fails to embody God's justice and righteousness (see Introduction, section 3, and especially 3b). If God is partial, God's partiality is for faithfulness and integrity that result in justice and *shalom* (see Introduction, section 4).

That Abimelech is, for all practical purposes, killed by "a certain woman" recalls the death of Sisera, who also was killed by a woman, Jael (Judg. 4—5). The parallel emphasizes again the deteriorating situation in the book of Judges. Sisera was a Canaanite military commander, while Abimelech is an Israelite. As suggested above, the threat from within can be just as dangerous as the threat from without. As noted previously, women play major roles in the book of Judges; and the nameless woman in 9:53 is no exception. But at this turning point in the book of Judges, she will be nearly the last woman to play an exemplary role (although see Samson's mother in Judges 13). Increasingly, as things grow worse among the Israelites, women will be victims rather than heroes (see commentary on chaps. 19—21; also Introduction, section 3d).

Abimelech's request to be finished off by his armor-bearer is similar to Saul's later request, so as to avoid dishonor (see 1 Sam. 31:4). Thus, the careers of Israel's first self-made king, Abimelech, and first divinely designated king, Saul, end in disgrace. Abimelech is an idolater from the beginning, and Saul is rejected by God for disobeying God's explicit command (1 Sam. 15). In the unfolding drama of God's involvement with Israel, God will be searching for a leader who will actually embody what Gideon had only articulated: "the LORD will rule over you" (8:23). It will not happen in the book of Judges; and it happened only fleetingly during the monarchy, which also would collapse under the weight of disobedience. From the Christian point of view, the search is completed only in King Jesus, who both proclaimed and embodied the good news that God alone rules over us.

75

10:1–5

Tola and Jair: The Calm between the Storms

After the brief but turbulent and tumultuous rule of Abimelech, the rather lengthy and comparatively uneventful careers of Tola and Jair are a welcome relief. There is another list of so-called minor judges in 12:8–15 (see Introduction, section 2a). It follows another turbulent episode, the violence between Jephthah and the men of Ephraim, in which 42,000 of the Ephraimites are killed (12:1–6). Thus, there seems to be a pattern that begins with the story of Gideon, which is a pivotal turning point in the book of Judges (see above). Each major judge's administration concludes with or is followed by Israelite-on-Israelite violence. The first two cycles are quite similar. Gideon (chaps. 6—8) is followed by Abimelech's violent rule (chap. 9), and then there is a respite (10:1–5). Jephthah's administration (10:6—12:7) ends in civil war (12:1–6), and then there is another respite (12:8–15). Samson's career (chaps. 13—16) is followed by more violence, including a bloody civil war (chaps. 17—21); but this time there is no relief. The book of Judges ends in chaos.

This pattern effectively communicates that things are getting worse among the Israelites. Persistent unfaithfulness and disobedience produce increasingly violent and chaotic results. Amid the progressive deterioration, however, stand the two lists of minor judges like two little oases in an increasingly expansive wasteland. Given Abimelech's slaughter of his seventy rivals and Jephthah's killing of his own daughter, it is refreshing and somewhat encouraging to read that Jair had thirty sons, none of whom were killed or even threatened, apparently (10:3–5). And Abdon, the final judge in the second list of minor judges, tops Jair; he has forty sons and thirty grandsons, all of whom survive, it seems (12:13–15).

To be sure, these details could be ancient historical remembrances with no great significance. It is entirely possible that the shapers of the book of Judges included the two lists of minor judges just to attain a total of twelve, one for each tribe. Even so, the pattern mentioned above suggests the possibility of some intentionality. For instance, the two lists of minor judges frame Jephthah's story; and it is difficult not to notice the contrast between Jair's and Abdon's extensive families and Jephthah's single daughter, whom he kills. From a purely narrative perspective, these details add poignancy to an already wrenching story.

The reports of extensive progeny may also suggest a possible theological function of 10:1–5 and 12:8–15. Elsewhere in the Old Testament, children are gifts of God; they indicate God's blessing. Thus, amid the increasingly chaotic and violent stories that indicate the Israelites are abandoning God, the two lists of minor judges suggest that God is not abandoning the Israelites (see 2:1, where God says, "I will never break my covenant with you."). Thus, even though only Tola, the first of the judges listed in 10:1–5 and 12:8–15, is said to "deliver Israel" (10:1), the stability and progeny communicated by the two lists suggest that God is still present among and faithful to God's covenant people. (For a different assessment of the role of 10:1–5, see Schneiders, 158, who suggests that 10:1–5 and 12:8–15 "continue to reflect a decline in the role of the judge . . . because they do not change any of the previous problems but maintain the status quo.")

If, as Claus Westermann argues, the function of God's saving activity is to restore the conditions that make normal daily life possible, then the normalcy communicated by the two lists of minor judges indicates that not even Israel's growing unfaithfulness and disobedience will fully or easily thwart God's purposes for life (Westermann, 45). Even when things seem to fall completely apart in Judges 17—21, this conclusion to the book of Judges anticipates God's further attempt to confront the chaos and to direct the existence of Israel so that life will again be possible (see 1 Sam. 1—8).

10:6—12:7
Jephthah and His Daughter: The Agony of Victory

If Israel's downhill slide began with Gideon, it clearly continues with Jephthah. Things are getting worse as the book of Judges proceeds, and the signs of decline are similar to those evident in the story of Gideon. The pattern that characterizes the book of Judges is evident, but it is again considerably altered (10:6–16). Like Gideon, Jephthah is an unlikely hero who gets off to a good start (10:17—11:28). But Jephthah's victory is tragically flawed by an apparently needless and senseless vow that results in the death of his only child, a daughter (11:29–40). Like Gideon, Jephthah has to deal with disgruntled Ephraimites; but the outcome in this case is a costly civil war (12:1–6). The downward spiral is signified by the short span of Jephthah's judging of Israel, as well as by the failure to achieve any "rest" for the land (12:7).

10:6–16 How Much Can God Stand?

As suggested above, the pattern that characterizes the book of Judges is evident from the beginning of Jephthah's story, as the people "again did what was evil in the sight of the LORD" (10:6; see 2:11; 3:7, 12; 4:1; 6:1; 13:1). But the description of the people's "evil" is noticeably intensified. Not surprisingly, the "Baals and the Astartes" are mentioned; but there follows a virtual catalogue of surrounding nations whose gods the people are worshiping instead of worshiping the LORD.

In keeping with the pattern, Israel is "sold" (10:7; see 2:4; 3:8; 4:2). But this time there are two oppressors—the Philistines and the Ammonites—only the latter of which will be dealt with by Jephthah. The Philistines remain a threat, and even Samson, the final judge, will only "begin to deliver Israel from the hand of the Philistines" (13:5). Things are getting worse.

A triad of verbs in verses 8–9 summarizes the seriousness of the situation—"crushed," "oppressed," and "distressed." The first of these occurs elsewhere only in Exodus 15:6 to describe what God had done to the Egyptians (NRSV "shattered"), but now the Israelites are on the receiving end. The second verb has occurred only recently in the book of Judges to describe what had happened to Abimelech when God "repaid" (9:56) him for his oppressive ways (see 9:53; NRSV "crushed"). But again, the Israelites are now the recipients of the action. The third verb recalls Judges 2:15, the first statement of the pattern in the book of Judges, where also the "distress" is precipitated by the people's idolatry.

Continuing the pattern, the people again "cried to the LORD" (10:10; see 3:9, 15; 4:3; 6:7); but this time, the content of their cry is different. Instead of a complaint about their suffering, the people offer a confession of sin. But it seems that their change of heart has come too late. God seems to have had enough, and God is not inclined to stand for any more: "therefore I will deliver you no more" (v. 13). But, when the people persist in their confession of sin, throw themselves upon God's mercy, and change their ways (vv. 15–16), God does proceed to deliver them by way of Jephthah, whose story begins in 11:1. In essence, God does not follow through with what God had announced in v. 13. Such "inconsistency" on God's part, however, is not really new. In Exodus 32:9–10, for instance, God announced the intention to destroy the people on account of their idolatry; but when Moses interceded, God "changed his mind about the disaster that he planned to bring on his people" (Exod. 32:14). Given the fact that Gideon's idolatrous behavior in 8:24–27 had recalled Exodus 32:1–14, it is not surprising that 10:16

should recall this pivotal text as well. The apparent "inconsistency" actually manifests the deeper divine consistency—that is, God is fundamentally "merciful and gracious" (Exod. 34:6). As suggested previously, the pervasive pattern in the book of Judges serves to communicate God's essential graciousness. To a people who repeatedly sin, God is repeatedly gracious (see Introduction, section 4).

This seems to be the meaning of the concluding clause of 10:16, at least as NRSV construes it: "and he could no longer bear to see Israel suffer." But NRSV has provided an uncharacteristically periphrastic translation at this point. The clause is quite ambiguous, and it could be translated more literally in the following possible ways:

. . . and his soul/life was shortened by the suffering of Israel.
. . . and his soul/life was shortened by the mischief of Israel.

The idiom of one's life/soul being shortened elsewhere communicates discouragement or impatience (see Num. 21:4; Mic. 2:7). This possible meaning seems to fit best with the divine announcement in verse 13 of no more deliverance.

On the other hand, the unfolding narrative reveals God's use of Jephthah to deliver Israel, at least from a portion of the threat. So, perhaps, the idiom here communicates God's merciful compassion, as NRSV suggests. This possible meaning can also claim the support of the larger canonical context, including the recurring pattern within the book of Judges itself as well as a pivotal text like Exodus 32—34.

Actually, the ambiguity of the clause is appropriate and instructive. The people's persistent disobedience, in the form of idolatrous self-assertion, certainly must discourage God and try God's patience; and yet God proves the divine character to be consistently gracious in continuing to put up with sinful people. In short, the ambiguity articulates, finally, God's suffering, consisting of God's ability and God's willingness to bear the burden of remaining faithfully in relationship with a persistently faithless people. This suggests another possible nuance of the idiom. God's "life is shortened"—that is, God's quality of life is diminished, or God suffers—as a result of the people's persistent unfaithfulness. (See Fretheim, *The Suffering of God*, 107–87; he points out that God regularly suffers *with* and *because of* the people; see his discussion of Judg. 10:16 on p. 129.)

As the larger biblical story continues to unfold, God will continue to have God's quality of life diminished by human sin. In other words, for love's sake God will continue to suffer—indeed, from a Christian perspective, all the way to the cross. The cross is the ultimate divine act

79

of *kenosis,* emptying or voluntary life-shortening for the sake of sinful people (see Introduction, section 4).

10:17—11:28 From Outlaw to Diplomat

The book of Judges is full of unlikely heroes—from left-handed Ehud, to the apparently non-Israelites Shamgar and Jael, to female Deborah, to Gideon, who was "the least" in his family (6:16). So, at this point in the book, the reader is not unduly surprised to learn that the next judge, Jephthah, was "the son of a prostitute" (11:1) and that he was forced into exile by his family and became the ancient equivalent of what today might be called a guerrilla fighter or terrorist. The key word in 10:17—11:11 is "head" (10:17; 11:8, 9, 11), which in other contexts can mean "first." Like Gideon's story, Jephthah's story involves "the least" or last becoming first. It's the way God typically works (see commentary on 6:1–32).

For the outcast son of a prostitute, Jephthah proves to be a rather skilled negotiator. He bargains carefully with the elders of Gilead to ensure that if God gives him the victory over the Ammonites, he will remain as the "head" over Gilead (11:4–11). Having successfully handled domestic policy, Jephthah turns his attention to foreign affairs, the Ammonite threat (11:12–28); and he again displays impressive diplomatic skills. Given the widespread impression that the book of Judges is a book of unmitigated violence, it is particularly important to note that Jephthah begins by attempting to establish peaceful relations with the Ammonites (12:12). When his initial question is met with an objection by the Ammonite king (12:13), Jephthah offers a detailed rehearsal of Numbers 21, explaining why Israel has a legitimate claim to some of the territory east of the Jordan (12:14–23).

Jephthah's argument leads up to the crucial questions in verse 24, which are again worthy of special notice, given the widespread impression that the book of Judges represents a sort of indiscriminate land-grab sponsored by Israel's God. To the contrary, Jephthah—and by implication, the God of Israel—recognizes that other peoples have legitimate claims to land and livelihood (see Deut. 32:8–9). Problems arise when any people wants too much, as the Ammonites do, in this case. As verse 24 suggests, the God of Israel wills nothing short of peaceful coexistence among all peoples and nations, which will result in the availability of land and livelihood for all. The larger context of the prophetic canon supports this perspective (see Introduction, section 3). When *any* nation or people—the Moabites, the Canaanites, the Midianites, the Ammonites, the Philistines, *or the Israelites*—overstep

God's good intentions, God stands against them! The downward spiral in the book of Judges is a warning about the inevitably negative consequences of persistent disobedience; and, of course, the larger prophetic canon narrates that Israel and Judah eventually fell as a result of their idolatrous self-assertion. But, with an insight growing out of the people's experience of disastrous consequences of their own actions, the prophetic canon also envisions that Israel will be "a light to the nations" (Isa. 42:6; 49:6), an agent of God's work of establishing justice and peace "for many peoples" (Isa. 2:4).

Although Judges 11:24 anticipates this direction of the larger prophetic canon, for now the Ammonite king rebuffs Jephthah's peace initiatives. For now, there will be war (11:27–28). One other detail of 11:24 should be noted. The god Chemosh is ordinarily the god of Moab, not the Ammonites, although Moab and Ammon are frequently associated (see Judg. 3:13–14; Gen. 19:36–38; Deut. 2:17–19). The apparent discrepancy does not really affect the substance of Jephthah's argument in verse 24; however, the allusion to the god of the Moabites may serve to call to mind 2 Kings 3:26–27, where the king of Moab sacrificed "his firstborn son" and turned the tide of battle against Israel to Moab's advantage (Olson, 830–31). If so, the allusion is a haunting anticipation of the next episode in Jephthah's story.

11:29–40 Keeping a Vow, Killing a Daughter

Up to this point, the story of Jephthah has gone well. The Israelites have confessed their sin and turned back to God, who, although frustrated by the people's fickle faith, remains committed to them (10:6–16). As one of the least, Jephthah seems to be God's kind of leader; and indeed he has made every attempt to establish the kind of peace among peoples and nations that God wills (10:17—11:28). At 11:29, however, Jephthah's story takes a tragic turn for the worse.

The beginning of verse 29 seems auspicious enough: "the spirit of the LORD came upon Jephthah." But the record of the spirit's effectiveness in the book of Judges is mixed. When the spirit came upon Othniel, the first judge, the result was an immediate victory (3:10–11). When the spirit possessed Gideon, however, Gideon proved to be hesitant, and he remained fearful (see 6:34 and the commentary on 6:33—8:3). The spirit will also come upon Samson. Its results will be impressive, but will not figure at all in the deliverance of Israel (see 14:6, 19; 15:14). This progression from immediate effectiveness (Othniel) to delayed effectiveness (Gideon) to virtually no effectiveness (Samson) is congruent with the progressive deterioration that characterizes the

81

book of Judges (see Introduction, section 2c), and it also provides a context for hearing 11:29–40.

The spirit may be an effective power; but it seems that it is not automatically effective, at least not in terms of effecting deliverance. The spirit comes upon or possesses human beings; therefore, it must be embodied with cooperation and faithfulness if deliverance is to be effected (see also commentary on 13:1–25, including the quotation from Richard G. Bowman; and commentary on 14:1—15:20). The progression from Othniel to Samson suggests diminishing faithfulness on the part of the judges upon whom the spirit comes. And, as suggested above, this diminishing faithfulness is paralleled by diminishing returns, in terms of deliverance. Othniel was completely effective, whereas Samson will only "begin to deliver Israel" (13:5). In between, Gideon does effect deliverance; but he also leads the people immediately back into idolatry (see commentary on 8:4–33), and he leaves a terribly violent legacy (see commentary on chap. 9). Jephthah too effects at least a partial deliverance by subduing the Ammonites (11:32–33), but the immediate result of his victory is violence—first, the death of his daughter as a result of his vow (11:34–40), and then a bloody civil war (12:1–6).

This pattern of progressive deterioration has a bearing on how Jephthah's vow in vv. 30–31 should be understood. In particular, it supports Phyllis Trible's conclusion:

> The making of the vow is an act of unfaithfulness. Jephthah desires to bind God rather than embrace the gift of the spirit. What comes to him freely, he seeks to earn and manipulate. The meaning of his words is doubt, not faith; it is control, not courage. To such a vow the deity makes no reply. (Trible, 97)

In short, Jephthah's response to the gift of God's spirit is similar to Gideon's. Gideon immediately doubted and devised a test for God (6:36–40). So too, although in a different manner, Jephthah doubts and devises a further means to attempt to guarantee victory.

To be sure, some commentators suggest that the spirit could have led Jephthah to make the vow. The text is sparse and thus ambiguous, but the book's pattern of progressive deterioration favors the conclusion that Jephthah's vow was unnecessary and unfaithful. Commentators have tried, too, to give Jephthah the benefit of the doubt, as it were, suggesting that in those days, he would reasonably have expected an animal to come out of the house rather than a person (NRSV "whoever" in v. 31 could also be translated "whatever"). But this direction of interpretation does not really help much. While animals may have lived in the house in those days, so did people! Jephthah, the smart and skilled negotiator of 11:12–28, surely should have foreseen all the possibilities. Thus, given the literary context, the attempt to give Jephthah the benefit of the doubt only makes him look worse—stupid and thoughtless, as well as unfaithful.

In any case, the vow is made to sacrifice whatever/whoever comes out of the house first (vv. 30–31); the Ammonites are subdued (vv. 32–33); and Jephthah comes home (v. 34). It was apparently customary after a victory for women to lead the celebration "with timbrels and dancing" (v. 34; see Exod. 15:20 and especially 1 Sam. 18:6). Had Jephthah forgotten this? We do not know. But in keeping with the apparent custom, a woman comes out first; and it is his daughter. What or whom did Jephthah expect? Again, we do not know. Given the custom and given that the daughter "was his only child" (v. 34), it does not seem that Jephthah should have been so surprised. But he obviously is surprised, as verse 35 suggests, and devastated. His actions bespeak his grief—"he tore his clothes"—as do his words (v. 35).

As several commentators point out, the story is narrated in such a way as to make Jephthah look as blameless as possible (see Fuchs, and see Exum 1989). Not only is he appropriately grief-stricken (v. 35), but also his daughter is completely supportive of her father: "[D]o to me according to what has gone out of your mouth" (v. 36). And later, in language that seems intentionally to evade the horror of the deed, it is reported that Jephthah "did with her according to the vow he had made" (v. 39).

Undoubtedly, the text reflects the arrangements of a patriarchal culture in which women were subordinate, marginalized, and manipulated. And it also reflects the typical reality that the marginalized have little choice but to comply. Even so, the text does not simply let Jephthah get away with murder. Granted, the details of the story itself seem to excuse the deed. And granted, commentators have often even commended Jephthah for being a man of his word, putting God first by keeping his vow even when it meant great cost to himself, his future, and his family, especially his daughter. But *context* is crucial; and both the immediate context of 11:29–40 within the book of Judges and the larger canonical context suggest that 11:29–40 may well have been a "text of terror" to ancient readers of the book of Judges just as much as it is to contemporary interpreters with feminist (or simply humane) sensitivities. As suggested above, the pattern of progressive deterioration—especially in texts involving the spirit of the LORD—makes Jephthah's vow suspect from the beginning. If the vow itself was "an act of unfaithfulness," as Trible puts it, then there is certainly no virtue in the

83

fulfillment of the vow. To commend Jephthah for being a man of his word because he fulfills his vow amounts to saying that it does not matter what one believes as long as one is sincere. To be sure, this seems to be a prevalent attitude among contemporary persons; but it is dangerous, and it is certainly misguided from a biblical perspective.

Although the narrated details of the story itself seem intended to absolve Jephthah, these details *in their present context* come off sounding ludicrous. For instance, Jephthah's words in verse 35—"you have become the cause of great trouble to me"—emphatically place the blame on his daughter! How unfair, and indeed, how ludicrous, given that Jephthah is the one who has uttered the unnecessary, unfaithful vow. What Jephthah eventually does is to sacrifice his daughter, an act that is specifically forbidden in the Torah (Lev. 18:21; 20:2–5) and criticized as well in the larger prophetic canon (2 Kgs. 23:10; Jer. 32:35). To be sure, the story in 11:29–40 may have originated *before* the promulgation of the Levitical codes and before the prophetic witness; but, *in its present context,* which assumes the giving of the Torah at least, Jephthah's sacrifice of his daughter is clearly a violation of God's purposes. (The dating of portions of 11:29–40 is debated. Thomas C. Römer, for instance, citing King Agamemnon's sacrifice of his daughter, Iphigenia, in some versions of the Iphigenia traditions, argues that Judg. 11:30–32, 39–40 are Persian or Hellenistic additions to the book of Judges that are designed to show that Jewish stories could be as tragic as the Greek classics.) What Jephthah did may have been acceptable to Molech (see Lev. 18:21; 20:2–5), the Ammonite god, but not to the God of Israel.

Interestingly, it is the Ammonites that Jephthah has defeated. Jephthah's story in its present canonical context thus has the effect of portraying Jephthah as a faithful Ammonite rather than a faithful Israelite! That is to say, Jephthah has done what idolaters do, not what faithful Israelites are called to do. Given that the problem portrayed in 10:6–16, the introduction to Jephthah's story, is precisely idolatry, this makes Jephthah's deed look all the more terrible (and casts him in the role of repeating Gideon's turn for the worse in 8:4–33).

When Jephthah's deed is heard in the context of 10:6–16 and 10:17–28, there are still other ways in which Jephthah looks bad. In 10:6–16 *God* had changed God's mind about not delivering the people anymore. If God's mind can change for the sake of graciously allowing people to live, why cannot Jephthah change his mind? At other places in the Old Testament, God even breaks the Torah in order to allow the people to live—for instance, inviting an adulterous people to return instead of killing them (see Jer. 3:11–14), and allowing Israel, the disobedient child, to be spared rather than stoned (see Hos. 11:1–9). In Jephthah's case, Jephthah could actually have appealed to the Torah as support for not sacrificing his child. But he does not. Where are the imaginative diplomatic skills of 11:12–28, where Jephthah shows detailed awareness of Numbers 21, a Torah narrative?

To be sure, these arguments may seem unfair from an historical perspective. But again, when the narrative is heard *in its present literary setting,* including its immediate context in the book of Judges and the larger canonical context, Jephthah looks worse than bad. He looks like a full-fledged idolater who shows no awareness of the Torah's prohibition of child sacrifice, much less of the merciful character of God who in the book of Judges has repeatedly offered life to those who actually deserved to die.

The preceding treatment of Jephthah has assumed that he did offer his daughter as a burnt offering, in accordance with the vow. There is a long-standing and persistent Jewish and Christian exegetical tradition that does make Jephthah look more imaginatively faithful and compassionate. According to this view, Jephthah does not kill his daughter by presenting her as a burnt offering, but rather dedicates her to a life of celibacy. This exegetical tradition apparently originated in the medieval era with David Kimchi, a Jewish commentator; and it was adopted by Christian interpreters who could then cite Jephthah's daughter as a precedent for celibacy among female religious orders (for a thorough treatment of the history of interpretation of 11:29–40, see Marcus).

This line of interpretation has every appearance of being a rationalization, an attempt to mitigate the horror of this "text of terror." Even so, it must be admitted, as suggested above, that the text is sparse and thus ambiguous. Dennis Olson has a very helpful perspective on this aspect of the text's ambiguity:

> The effect of the ambivalence is to heighten suspense, to draw the reader into wrestling with the moral dilemmas and ambiguities of the story, and to increase the sense of horror at a possibility so repulsive that it is not described but left only as an imagined potentiality. . . . In the end, whether Jephthah's daughter was sacrificed or lived a life of celibacy, Jephthah's vow remains foolish, wrong, and unnecessary. (Olson, 834)

In short, Jephthah's treatment of his daughter is not to be commended on any grounds. Rather, his foolish, faithless act shows the horrible, terror-filled results of not enacting and embodying what God wills. Not surprisingly, Jephthah's violence against his daughter is multiplied excessively in 12:1–6. Both instances of violence demonstrate the progressive deterioration that characterizes the movement of the

85

book of Judges. Whereas women in the opening chapters of Judges are honored and even play leading roles—Achsah (1:11–15), Deborah, and Jael (chaps. 4—5)—women become increasingly manipulated and victimized. The treatment of Jephthah's daughter is a prime example, of course; but there will be further horror stories—the Levite's concubine (chap. 19), as well as the kidnappings of the four hundred women of Jabesh-gilead (21:8–12) and the women of Shiloh (21:15–24). Increasingly, the abuse of women demonstrates the violent results of failing to be faithful and obedient (see Introduction, section 3d).

The preceding treatment of 11:29–40 has implicated Jephthah for being faithless and disobedient, but what about God's role in the story? Some commentators attribute the tragedy to God's failure as much or more than to Jephthah's, especially when 11:29–40 is heard in conjunction with Genesis 22:1–19, the near sacrifice of Isaac. The story of Jephthah and his daughter clearly calls to mind the story of Abraham and his son, Isaac. This is especially the case in verse 34, where it is emphasized that Jephthah's daughter is his "only child" (see Gen. 22:2). In Genesis 22:1–19, God intervenes to prevent Abraham from sacrificing his only son; but there is no divine intervention to prevent the sacrifice of Jephthah's daughter. Why not? The point is not that God cares less about women than men. Rather, the literary and theo-logic of Judges 11:29–40 does not permit God to intervene. In Genesis 22:1–19, *God* proposes the test, not Abraham. In Judges 11:29–40, Jephthah proposes the vow, not God. Abraham's faithfulness in response to *God's* test shows that God does not will human sacrifice. Jephthah's unfaithfulness and *self*-assertiveness in sacrificing his daughter also show that God does not will human sacrifice. Especially when heard in its context, Judges 11:29–40 communicates the horrible results of faithlessness and disobedience. As such, it is, as the entire book of Judges is, a call to repentance and a call to covenant loyalty. The biblical God does not force the divine will upon us. God may be able to forgive Jephthah's— and our—unfaithfulness, injustice, and violence; but God cannot prevent it. The existence of injustice and violence in the world, then and now, does not mean that God is evil or absent. Rather, it means that God has lovingly entrusted humankind with dominion (see Gen. 1:26–31). As suggested above, Israel's—and our—unfaithfulness and disobedience hurt God and diminish God's quality of life. But, for love's sake, God remains faithful to God's unfaithful human partners.

Love requires freedom (see Hall, *God and Human Suffering,* 70–71). But the same freedom that allows Abraham—and us—to be faithful also allows Jephthah—and us—to be unfaithful. God's unwillingness, for love's sake, to coerce obedience does not mean that God is absent. But it does mean that we may have to look in unexpected places to locate God, in the world as well as in the story of Jephthah and his daughter. If, as suggested above, our unfaithfulness and disobedience hurt God as well as hurting other people, then we should locate God's presence in Judges 11:29–40 with the aggrieved and the grieving—that is, with Jephthah's daughter and with those who grieved in solidarity with her during her lifetime (11:37–38) and who kept her memory alive after her death (11:40).

The book of Judges is, in Marvin Tate's words, "a book of weeping" (see commentary on 1:1—2:5). The first introduction to the book of Judges ends with the people weeping (2:4) at a place called Bochim ("Weeping"), because the angel of the LORD has warned them of the disastrous consequences of their idolatry. Toward the end of the book of Judges, the Israelites weep again as a result of a bloody civil war (20:23, 26) and its aftermath (21:2). Because the book of Judges is framed by weeping over the results of idolatry and disobedience, it is not surprising that chapter 11—exactly the middle chapter of the book—also culminates in the weeping of Jephthah's daughter and her friends. Jephthah's daughter, although she remains nameless, is at least allowed to speak (unlike the Levite's concubine in chapter 19, who is both nameless and voiceless). Her speech is not just submissive (v. 36). Rather, she also claims enough initiative to request something from her father. And, given the book's framework of weeping, it is crucial note that Jephthah's daughter asks for time to "weep (over) my virginity" (v. 37; NRSV "bewail my virginity"). Then, it is reported that she and her friends "wept (over) her virginity." Recalling the opening of the book and anticipating its conclusion, this weeping at the heart of the book of Judges reinforces the conclusion that Jephthah's behavior partakes of idolatry, unfaithfulness, and disobedience. Although Jephthah's daughter was victimized by her father and has often been marginalized by the history of interpretation of the book of Judges, her story of weeping is at the very heart of this "book of weeping." The story of Jephthah's daughter and her friends serves as the graphic central panel of a work that illustrates the horror and violent inhumanity that inevitably result from idolatry and self-assertion—in short, from the *failure* to keep covenant.

Quite appropriately, therefore, Jephthah's daughter and her victimization become the occasion for an annual observance. The final phrase of verse 39 can be translated, "and she became a tradition in Israel" (Trible, 106). The primary activity of the observance or tradition is to "rehearse" or "proclaim" (v. 40; NRSV "lament") the daughter of Jephthah. The tone of the observance might well have been lament, but

87

the lament would have also proclaimed a message. Because to remember Jephthah's daughter and her weeping is to confront the horrible consequences of idolatry and disobedience, the tradition would have functioned as a call to repentance. This is not surprising, since the story of Jephthah's daughter lies at the heart of a book that is part of the prophetic canon.

A male-dominated history of interpretation has sometimes identified the judges, especially Samson, as types of Jesus. The logic goes something like this: as Samson was a powerful deliverer, so also Jesus was a powerful deliverer. But such logic is questionable, especially in the case of Samson, whose character was terribly flawed and who did not really accomplish deliverance for the people (see commentary on chaps. 13—16). If there is any type of Jesus in the book of Judges—that is, anyone who embodies God's experience—the most likely candidate is Jephthah's daughter.

Like God in the book of Judges, Jephthah's daughter is the victim of unfaithfulness and disobedience. In this way too, of course, Jephthah's daughter anticipates Jesus, another innocent victim of human unfaithfulness and disobedience. Like Jephthah's daughter, proclaiming and remembering Jesus' death became a custom or tradition for those whom he called friends or companions (literally, "eaters of bread with"). Both the death of Jephthah's daughter and the death of Jesus are described as sacrifices.

It is precisely at this point that the death of Jephthah's daughter might help Christians understand more fully the death of Jesus. In particular, the terror of Judges 11:29–40 may help Christians realize that the cross of Jesus Christ is also a horror story. Like Jephthah's daughter, Jesus was the victim of unfaithfulness and idolatry. To affirm this is also to affirm that suffering as such is not redemptive. The cross is a symbol of redemption because it demonstrates how much God loves the world and consequently how far God goes in giving of God's self for the sake of the sinful world. The point is love, not suffering. Love redeems, not suffering. To be sure, those who love will inevitably suffer. But the reverse is not true; not all suffering is evidence of love.

A misguided theology of the cross has often held that suffering itself is automatically virtuous and redemptive. On these grounds, Christian pastors have even counseled battered women to accept more suffering and abuse. In other words, the cross has been invoked to perpetuate injustice; and the effect has been to create more female victims like Jephthah's daughter. What Judges 11:29–40 can teach us is that suffering and "sacrifice" are not good when they result from idolatry and

88

unfaithfulness and thus perpetrate injustice. A biblical theology of the cross should also teach us this (see Cousar, 7–9, 52–87).

The resurrection of Jesus is a validation, not of the disobedience and unfaithfulness that killed him, but rather of the divine love that Jesus proclaimed and embodied in his life and ministry. We do not, of course, proclaim the resurrection of Jephthah's daughter; however, the daughters of Israel remembered and told of her, and we can and must do the same. And, as J. Cheryl Exum suggests, "To recount the story of Jephthah's daughter is to make her live again through words" (Exum, *Tragedy and Biblical Narrative,* 61).

What Elie Wiesel says of the Holocaust, the death of six million Jews at the hands of the Nazis (most of whom were professing Christians!), should be said too of the holocaust of Jephthah's daughter— namely, we cannot tolerate the silence of memory, lest it happen again. As Jephthah's daughter continued to live through the words of the daughters of Israel, and as she continues to live through our words, we call ourselves and the world to repentance for the unfaithfulness, disobedience, and injustice that tragically continue to be manifest in the abuse of children and women.

The Jewish Holocaust and the story of the holocaust of Jephthah's daughter are also timely reminders of how frequently inhumanity and violence are perpetrated in the name of God. Just because we invoke the name of God, as Jephthah did, does *not* mean that we are being faithful and obedient. It is entirely possible, as the Decalogue recognizes, to "make wrongful use of the name of the LORD your God" (Exod. 20:7). Jesus put it this way: "Not everyone who says to me, 'Lord, Lord,' will enter the kingdom of heaven, but only the one who does the will of my Father in heaven" (Matt. 7:21). As is shown in the death of Jephthah's daughter, revealed in the crucifixion of Jesus, and borne out in historical events like the Holocaust, it is far more difficult to be faithful than it is to attempt to cloak unfaithfulness in divine garb. To remember and proclaim Jephthah's daughter and to pick up a cross to follow Jesus is to have the faith and the courage to name idolatry and injustice, and for God's sake to pursue the difficult way of faithfulness and justice instead.

12:1–7 Jephthah's Violent Legacy

As suggested above, the stories of Gideon and Jephthah have significant parallels. Both start out well, but each takes a decided turn for the worse, resulting in a violent legacy. It is not surprising, therefore, that Jephthah is confronted by the Ephraimites with almost exactly the

89

same objection that the Ephraimites had voiced to Gideon (12:1; cf. 8:1). Given the circumstances, the threat made by the Ephraimites in 12:1 is particularly cruel. They threaten to "burn your house down over you," thus recalling for Jephthah the fiery sacrifice of his daughter that had already effectively destroyed Jephthah's "house" (that is, his family line).

Perhaps the cruelty of the Ephraimites elicits Jephthah's cruel response. In any case, and in marked contrast to Gideon's response to the Ephraimites, the formerly skilled negotiator (see above on 10:17–28) does not even give the Ephraimites a chance to respond. Instead, he immediately engages in battle against them. The famous Shibboleth-Sibboleth episode (12:5–6), which hinges on the alternative pronunciations of the next-to-last letter in the Hebrew alphabet, serves to emphasize the cruelty and magnitude of this Israelite-on-Israelite violence. The "massive defeat" (11:33) that Jephthah had inflicted on the Ammonites is now matched by his massive defeat of a tribe of his own people, in which 42,000 Ephraimites were killed (12:6).

There could hardly be a more dramatic indication that things are getting worse as the book of Judges proceeds. As it turns out, Jephthah's unnecessary, unfaithful vow that led to the death of his daughter was only the beginning of the tragedy. Readers of the book can only be thankful that Jephthah judged Israel only six years as compared to the longer administrations of previous judges (12:7). And, not surprisingly, there is no indication by the narrator that the land had "rest." In view of the death of Jephthah's daughter and then of 42,000 Ephraimites, it clearly did not! Thus the story of Jephthah, by graphically portraying the violent effects of unfaithfulness and idolatry, furthers the prophetic function of the entire book of Judges. For readers, ancient and contemporary, it invites consideration of how they/we may be complicit in idolatry and disobedience. It thus serves as a call to repentance and to faithful, righteous lives that renounce self-assertion in favor of the kind of costly grace that God demonstrates in response to God's people (see above on 10:6–16).

12:8–15

Ibzan, Elon, and Abdon: An Interlude of Blessing

As suggested in the comment on 10:1–5, it is possible that the material on the so-called minor judges is included in the book just to achieve a total of twelve judges, in which case 10:1–5 and 12:8–15 offer little in the way of theological significance. Even so, the pattern that begins with Gideon is noticeable—that is, each major judge's tenure (see chaps. 6—8; 10:6—11:40; 13—16) either ends with or is followed by violence (see chaps. 9; 12:1–7; 17—21). This pattern communicates the progressive deterioration that characterizes the book, suggesting that persistent idolatry and disobedience produce increasingly violent and chaotic conditions. Between the episodes of the last three major judges, however, stand the two lists of minor judges (see commentary on 10:1–5).

If this arrangement is not merely coincidental, then 10:1–5 and 12:8–15 may serve a narrative and even a theological function. As suggested above, the two units frame the material on Jephthah; and there is a marked contrast between the large families of Jair (10:3–5), Ibzan (12:8–10), and Abdon (12:13–15)—and Jephthah's single daughter. Adding poignancy to this narrative sequence is the notice that Ibzan "gave his thirty daughters in marriage outside his clan and brought in thirty young women from outside for his sons" (12:9). In sharp contrast, of course, Jephthah had killed his lone child; then he had proceeded to massacre thousands of people outside his clan.

The possible theological function of 10:1–5 and 12:8–15 is also related to the focus on children, who are viewed elsewhere in the Old Testament as signs of God's blessing. Placed as they are between the increasingly violent stories that indicate the Israelites' unfaithfulness to God, 10:1–5 and 12:8–15 affirm that God's faithfulness abounds despite Israel's unfaithfulness. If there is anything indicating that 12:8–15 participates in the pattern of progressive deterioration that characterizes the book of Judges, it is the relatively shorter administrations of Ibzan, Elon, and Abdon in comparison to Tola and Jair. Even so, the relative calm between the turbulent, tragic episodes of Jephthah and Samson suggests that not even Israel's growing idolatry and self-assertion will be able finally to thwart God's purposes for life.

If 12:8–15 plays this kind of theological role, then it should be noted that the pattern mentioned above is not completed within the book of Judges. That is, the Samson material is followed by violence, but there is no respite such as 10:1–5 and 12:8–15 provide following Gideon and Jephthah. The book of Judges ends in total chaos. From this perspective, the correlate of 10:1–5 and 12:8–15 must be found in 1 Samuel. Even after the life of Israel totally degenerates and the people nearly destroy themselves (Judg. 17—21), God will not abandon the people. First Samuel initiates a new strategy on God's part; but of course the monarchy will end in chaos just as the book of Judges does.

91

That will not be the end of the story either. As 10:1–5 and 12:8–15 affirm—and indeed as the repeated pattern throughout the book of Judges affirms—God simply will not give up on God's wayward people. To be sure, there are always destructive consequences for unfaithfulness and disobedience; but here, as always in Scripture, grace abounds.

13:1—16:31
Samson, His Mother, and His Lovers

The last and probably best known of the judges is Samson, although most people's knowledge of Samson is limited to his relationship with Delilah (16:4–31); and the source of people's knowledge is as likely to be Cecil B. DeMille's film *Samson and Delilah* as it is the biblical text. Samson's story contains all the features that make for a top-rated movie—excessive violence, romance and sex, and R-rated humor. No wonder it attracted DeMille!

Of course, Samson's story has long been recognized as a good one, and commentators quite properly have analyzed it from the perspective of folklore and traditional storytelling. James Crenshaw, for instance, concludes that Samson's story "demonstrates Israelite narrative art at its zenith" (Crenshaw, 149). Crenshaw and others point out that both ordinary readers and quite sophisticated readers have always been drawn to Samson's story—from the author of the Letter to the Hebrews (see 11:32), to early church fathers who saw Samson as a parallel to Hercules and as a type of Christ, to John Milton and his *Samson Agonistes* (see Crump), to Cecil B. DeMille.

When the story of Samson is approached from the perspective of folklore, Samson can be identified with certain typical figures in the Bible as well as in other ancient literature from a variety of cultures. Susan Niditch, for instance, describes Samson under the rubrics of "culture hero," "trickster," and "bandit." Characteristic of the "culture hero" are Samson's extraordinary birth (chapter 13) and the superhuman strength that he uses to oppose a traditional enemy, the Philistines. The "trickster" motif is especially evident in chapters 14—16, where several encounters and the resulting complications involve deception, riddles, and clever revenge. A related type is the "social bandit," who typically operates at the margins of society on behalf of an oppressed group, and who, though apparently invincible, dies in the end.

Although Robert Alter has called for scholars to move beyond folklore in order to appreciate the "moral" and artistic subtleties of the Samson story (see Alter), it is clear that Niditch already discerns a crucial moral dimension in Judges 13—16. She concludes, as follows:

> The overriding theme and concern . . . , whether Samson be viewed as culture hero, trickster, or bandit, is the marginal's confrontation with oppressive authority, more specifically Israel's dealings with its Philistine enemies. Scenes having to do with the birth of the hero, his adventures with women and assailants, and finally his death all emphasize the victory of the weak over seemingly implacable forces. . . . As such, the tale of Samson is a powerful statement of hope and vindication as well as a visceral comment on problems inherent in relations with the non-Israelite world. (Niditch, "Samson as Culture Hero," 624)

In other words, the story of Samson is about what the entire book of Judges is about—God's will to oppose cruel oppression and the difficulties involved in the actual embodiment of God's will by God's people, especially in a Canaanite context (see Introduction, section 4). While Samson certainly is a "hero" of sorts, his story comes at a point in the book of Judges that suggests that Samson is also the *worst* of the judges. Things have been getting progressively worse since Gideon; and after Samson, things degenerate into utter chaos. As the final judge, Samson represents not the glorious culmination of the series of judges, but rather its abysmal conclusion (see Introduction, section 2c). Although Samson's feats were impressive, and although he killed many Philistines, at best he only began to deliver Israel from the Philistine oppressor (see 13:5). At the end of Samson's life and his story, things are no better than they were before; and if chapters 17—21 are any indication, they are actually much worse.

If the story of Samson is a story about God's will, as suggested above, it is primarily about the difficulties involved in the achievement of God's will. God's will for the deliverance of the people is clear enough; but Samson's *unfaithfulness* is clear too, as he violates at every turn the Nazirite vow announced in 13:5. In a story full of riddles, perhaps the greatest riddle of all is that God can accomplish anything at all through a character like Samson, who, as James Wharton points out, "looks very much like an oversexed buffoon" (Wharton, 58).

To be sure, God did not accomplish much through him, as it turns out, although Samson did at least strike a blow at the Philistines—not actual deliverance, but at least a beginning (13:5). The incompleteness of Samson's story, and indeed the incompleteness of the entire book of Judges, is an invitation to hear the book of Judges in its larger canonical context, especially the context of the prophetic canon. The

93

prophetic canon bears witness to the ultimate riddle or mystery—that a God who fervently wills faithfulness, justice, and peace remains unfailingly committed to people whose persistent unfaithfulness and disobedience regularly result in chaos and destruction. In a word, of course, it is the riddle of grace. The story of Samson, the entire book of Judges, and the whole prophetic canon fully articulate God's fervent desire for the covenant loyalty that produces life as God intends it; they unflinchingly document the human unfaithfulness that yields chaos and destruction; and yet they affirm God's abiding presence and commitment amid the messes that God's people make. The prophetic books—including the book of Judges (and especially the book of Judges at its lowest point with Samson and the aftermath in chaps. 17—21)—are powerful statements of hope; not hope in "culture heroes" like Samson, but rather hope in a God whose grace is greater than our ability to comprehend and whose commitment to justice, righteousness, and peace surpasses our understanding.

13:1–25 The Mother of a Hero, or the Mother As a Hero?

The story begins as if it will display the typical pattern, as the Israelites again "did what was evil" and "the LORD gave them into the hand of the Philistines" (v. 1; see 2:11, 14; 3:7–8, 12; 4:1–2; 6:1; 10:7–8). But the pattern is immediately altered. The people do *not* cry out to God for help, either at this point in the story or at any other. While the narrator seems to recognize the Philistines as oppressors, the people do not. Indeed, later in the story the people seem perfectly content to acknowledge "that the Philistines are rulers over us" (15:11). This is not a good sign. At least Gideon had properly affirmed that "the LORD will rule over you" (8:23), even if his behavior immediately belied this affirmation. Now, however, the people seem to have no clue that God should be their ruler. If the problem in the book of Judges is the people's collaboration with the inhabitants of the land (see 2:2; 3:6), then the people have now reached a new low. They are completely acquiescent, to the point that their acknowledgment of Philistine rule is accompanied by their action to turn Samson, their potential deliverer, over to the Philistines (15:12–13).

In terms of the possible origins of the Samson story in the premonarchic era, perhaps the people of Judah turn Samson over to the Philistines because Samson is from Dan, and hence not one of their own men. But in terms of the canonical shape of the book, the people of God are supposed to be united in their allegiance to God and in their opposition to the people of the land (see 2:2; Josh. 24). From either the historical or the canonical perspective, disunity is the rule and deliverance is apparently out of the question.

But God is not finished with this unfaithful people. Even though they fail to cry out, God will be about deliverance. To be sure, it is not stated explicitly that God raised up a deliverer (see 2:16; 3:9, 15); but the story that begins in verse 2 will lead to the birth of a boy "who shall begin to deliver Israel" (v. 5). That the deliverance will not be complete is another indication that things have reached a new low. The problem will be not only the people's lack of faith and their acquiescence with Philistine rule (see above), but Samson himself will be none too faithful either. And if he does not exactly acquiesce with Philistine rule, his weakness for Philistine women will keep him in regular contact with the enemy. This will give him several opportunities to exact revenge, and he will kill many Philistines; but even his culminating triumph marks his own demise (16:28–31), and it does *not* involve the complete deliverance of Israel!

If Samson is a hero, therefore, he is clearly a flawed hero. He is so busy pursuing his attraction to Philistine women and taking personal revenge on the Philistines that he shows little interest in or inclination toward delivering Israel. Even the culmination of the story is as much a matter of personal revenge as anything else (see 16:28). Although Samson does finally implore God for help (see also 15:18–20), the strength that God grants leads to a rather hollow victory—Samson's death and no deliverance.

Therefore, if there is a truly faithful hero in the story, it appears to be not Samson but rather Samson's mother. She, not he, is the model of faithfulness, attentiveness to God and God's word, and just plain good sense (see v. 23). Not surprisingly, chapter 13 is devoted largely to Samson's parents, Manoah and his unnamed wife. Given the major role played by Samson's mother, something not unusual for a woman in the book of Judges (see Introduction, section 3d), it is surprising that she remains unnamed. Two other major female characters in the book of Judges are unnamed, Jephthah's daughter (11:29–40) and the Levite's concubine (chap. 19). In these cases, being unnamed seems to designate marginalization and victimization; but this cannot be the case in chapter 13, since Samson's mother clearly comes off looking better than her bumbling husband, and since she is apparently both attentive and faithful to the divine revelation that she has been honored to receive.

Perhaps another riddle posed by the text is this: Why does Samson's mother remain unnamed? According to Robert Alter, this "namelessness of Samson's mother is beautifully convenient because every

95

time she is involved in speech or action she can be referred to as 'the woman,'" a word that Alter has previously identified as thematic for the story of Samson (Alter, 51). Thus, for Alter, chapter 13 effectively anticipates other references to the women in Samson's story (see 14:1–2; 16:1, where "prostitute" is literally "a woman of whoredom"; and 16:4). Furthermore, the role reversal—the unnamed woman is clearly the more positive character in comparison to her clueless husband—conforms to similar role reversals in the book of Judges, where women occupy the traditional male roles (see especially Deborah and Jael in chaps. 4—5, and the woman who kills Abimelech in 9:53; see also the Introduction, section 3d).

Adele Reinhartz has proposed another possible solution that has affinities with the notion of role reversal. She suggests that the namelessness of Samson's mother be heard in the light of the angel's refusal to divulge a name (vv. 17–18). The mutual namelessness stresses the intimacy between the angel and Samson's mother, and it thus serves to emphasize the central role of Samson's mother.

> As a being sent by God, the angel's name cannot be divulged. Though the woman herself is not divine, she has encounters with and knowledge of a divine being, contacts that are far superior in quantity and quality to that between her and her named and very human spouse. Her son also, though named by the woman and divinely promised, demonstrates his all-too-human failings in the rest of the Samson saga, and therefore does not live up to expectations in his role as judge and potential savior from Philistine control. (Reinhartz, 29)

Reinhartz's conclusion reinforces the proposal made above that Samson's mother is the real hero of the Samson story, and herein may lie another hidden riddle in a text that is full of overt riddles. In other words, will the reader of Judges 13—16 have the insight to detect that of all the characters in Judges 13—16, an unnamed woman bears the closest relationship to God and models the behavior that God wills for God's people throughout the book of Judges—attentiveness to God's word and a distinctive lifestyle that sets one apart from other nations and their destructive ways?

The angelic announcement, of course, was meant to set Samson apart as well; but Samson paid no attention whatsoever to his distinctive Nazirite status (see below). If he had heeded the words (see 14:3) and example of his mother, including her faithfulness and her good sense, perhaps Samson might have avoided botching the office of judge and thus bringing the office of judge (at least within the book of Judges) to a dramatic but ignominious conclusion. In any case, the reader is encouraged to see Samson's mother not simply as the mother of a hero,

but rather *as a hero,* the one character in Judges 13—16 who exemplifies faithfulness to God's word and God's ways. Readers have regularly
failed to discern this reality and have instead been inclined to view Samson, the "oversexed buffoon," as the hero of the story—so easy is it to
be misled by appearances and by impressive though ineffectual displays
of power. The role reversal performed by Judges 13, and indeed by the
portrayal of women elsewhere in the book of Judges, anticipates the
role reversals performed by Jesus and his announcement and embodiment of the reign of God, in which the last shall be first and the greatest among us will be a servant. Not unlike Judges 13, Jesus had a way
of making unnamed women into heroes (see Mark 14:3–9).

If, as H. R. Jauss maintains, the aesthetic value of a literary work is
highest when it frustrates or disappoints the expectations of its readers,
then the story of Samson is an aesthetic masterpiece (see Reinhartz,
25). There is every indication in chapter 13 that Samson will be a hero,
including the following elements, which will be discussed in turn below:
(1) the angel's appearance and announcement to a barren woman, (2)
the Nazirite vow, and (3) the blessing by God associated with the "spirit
of the LORD" (vv. 24–25). Thus, perhaps it is understandable that less-
than-alert readers have been misled, failing to see that Samson disappoints these expectations, and thus failing to discern the riddle that
Samson's mother is the truly faithful hero.

That Samson's father is mentioned first and by his name, Manoah,
is typical of a patriarchal context; but it may also be another little trick
of the narrator to set up an expectation that will be disappointed. The
major characters in chapter 13 are Manoah's unnamed wife (see above)
and the angel of the LORD. That Manoah's wife is barren and is
promised a child immediately calls to mind other barren women and
the divine promises made to them: Sarah (Gen. 11:30; 18:9–15; 21:1–7),
Rebekah (Gen. 25:21–26), Rachel (Gen. 29:31; 30:22–24; 35:16–20),
and Hannah (1 Sam. 1:1–28). The sons of these women are among the
most important and heroic of Old Testament figures: Isaac, Jacob,
Joseph, and Samuel.

Although Samson's mother dutifully reports to her husband the
appearance of the angel and his announcement (vv. 6–7) and comes to
get her husband when the angel returns (v. 10), she is clearly the more
alert and intelligent actor in the story. The angel, in effect, puts Manoah
in his place when he tells him to listen to what his wife has already told
him (vv. 12–14). Although Manoah's concern about seeing God reflects
a tradition evident elsewhere in the Old Testament (v. 20; see Gen.
32:30; Exod. 33:20), his fear is comically out of proportion; and his wife's
reasonable and perceptive response puts the matter to rest. Amid the

97

comical interactions among Manoah, his wife, and the angel, however, there are other Old Testament allusions that heighten the reader's expectations for Samson. Verses 15–20 recall Abraham and his hospitality to the messengers who announced to him that Sarah would bear a son (Gen. 28:1–15), as well as Jacob's request to know the name of the "man" with whom he wrestled all night (Gen. 32:22–32, especially v. 29).

These allusions lead the reader to expect that the child to be born, Samson, will have the same significance as Abraham, Isaac, and Jacob— that is, at a crucial point when the future of God's people is threatened, Samson will be the one to facilitate the creation, or re-creation, of the people. The angel's response to Manoah's inquiry about his name reinforces these high hopes (v. 18). His name, says the angel, is "too wonderful"; and Manoah subsequently offers a sacrifice to the God who is "working wonders" (v. 19; see NRSV note). The repeated Hebrew root in verses 18–19 is *pl'*. It echoes Gen. 18:14, in the context of the announcement that God will cause Sarah to have a son; and it also regularly designates the "wonders" that God does in effecting deliverance (see Exod. 3:20; 15:11; Josh. 3:5; Judg. 6:13). Again, every indication is that Samson will be a heroic deliverer.

Then too, this expectation is reinforced by the announcement that the son to be born "shall be a nazirite to God from birth" (v. 5). As the NRSV note indicates, the word "nazirite" means "one separated" or "one consecrated." Given that Israel's problem is idolatry and disobedience, manifest especially in their collaboration with the inhabitants of Canaan (see 2:1–5), the people seem especially to need a leader who will be "one separated," one distinctively set apart for service to God and able to lead others in this direction. This need would have been all the more urgent at this point in the book of Judges, given the turn for the worse that started with Gideon and the progressive deterioration that has continued with Jephthah (see Introduction, section 2c, and commentary on chaps. 6—8 and 10:6—12:7, especially on 8:4–33; 11:29–40; 12:1–7). At a point in the book when the Israelites have fully acquiesced with Philistine rule and when deliverance seems out of the question (15:9–13; see above), extraordinary measures are necessary.

This may explain not only why the next leader needs to be a Nazirite, but also why the Nazirite vow is not just the temporary consecration envisioned and described in Numbers 6:1–21. The crisis is of such magnitude that a *lifelong* Nazirite is needed, so Samson is to "be a nazirite to God from birth" (v. 5). When Samson's mother conveys the angel's announcement to her husband, she adds that Samson "shall be a nazirite to God from birth to the day of his death," thus emphasizing the lifelong status. As many commentators point out, this elaboration upon the angel's message anticipates Samson's dramatic death in chapter 16 (due, of course, to his unfaithfulness to the Nazirite vow). It is not necessary to conclude, as Mieke Bal does, that the added words of Samson's mother have the effect of condemning her son to death (Bal, 31, 74–75). If there is any significance to the elaboration in verse 7 other than to emphasize the lifelong Nazirite status and perhaps to allude to chapter 16, then it is probably also to anticipate the next major leader of Israel—namely, Samuel, whose mother also sets him apart as a Nazirite before his birth (although not under divine direction) and promises God that he will be "a nazirite until the day of his death" (1 Sam. 1:11).

That Samuel, the very next leader in the canonical sequence, needs also to be a lifelong Nazirite, and that his first order of business is dealing with the ongoing Philistine threat (see 1 Sam. 4:1), is further testimony to Samson's failure. To be sure, the narrator has alerted the reader to what will be Samson's failure by way of the verb "begin" in verse 5; however, readers have regularly missed this clue, and they thus have persisted in interpreting Samson as a hero, and as suggested above, even as a prefigurement of Christ. Careful attention to verse 5, as well as an appreciation of the context of Judges 13—16 in the book of Judges and in the larger prophetic canon, will lead the reader to recognize that almost everything Samson does in chapters 14—16 is a violation of his Nazirite status. To be sure, it is possible that chapter 13 is a later addition to earlier stories about Samson and his feats; but this is a problematic conclusion, because chapter 13 contains necessary information for understanding the significance of Samson's hair in chapter 16. In any case, in the final form of chapters 13—16, especially when heard within their immediate and larger context, Samson could hardly look worse.

Every element of his Nazirite status will be violated. Sampson apparently does not shun "wine and strong drink" (see 14:5, 10; cf. Num. 6:3); he does not avoid contact with a carcass (see 14:8; cf. Num. 6:6–8); and finally, he foolishly allows his hair to be cut (see 16:15–22; cf. Num. 6:5–6). Then too, of course, Samson is in regular contact (quite literally!) "with the inhabitants of this land" (2:2), something prohibited from the beginning by the book of Judges (2:1–5; see 3:6). In fact, the remainder of Samson's story is best organized around his encounters with three Philistine women—the woman from Timnah (14:1—15:20), the prostitute in the Philistine city of Gaza (16:1–3), and Delilah (16:4–31).

99

Before turning to chapters 14—16 and Samson's (mis)deeds, however, it is necessary to consider a final aspect of chapter 13 that heightens the sense of expectation surrounding Samson. After the actual account of the birth of Samson, the narrator relates the following: "the LORD blessed him. The spirit of the LORD began to stir him" (vv. 24–25). This sounds quite promising; however, the repetition of the verb "begin," echoing verse 5, should perhaps put the reader on alert. In chapters 14—16, there is ample evidence that Samson is "blessed"; or as James C. Howell puts it in "The Primrose Path of Dalliance," "the first thing we can say about Samson is that he is *gifted*" (emphasis added). The real question, however, is what Samson *does* with his gifts or blessings. At the end of chapter 13, this remains to be seen; and chapters 14—16 will suggest that Samson's gifts are used primarily for the pursuit of Philistine women and for exacting personal revenge upon the Philistines who attempt to thwart his purposes.

In short, as Richard G. Bowman points out in assessing Judges 13—16 and the entire book of Judges, being "blessed" by God and being gifted by "the spirit of the LORD" are no guarantee that the person will fulfill *God's* purposes.

> Although the narrator of Judges portrays God as actively intervening in the life of the Hebrew people, the narrator shows God acting without constraint with complete success only when authorizing punishment for human transgressions. The narrator's portrayal also shows God intervening to initiate a process of deliverance from oppression. The initial step in this process is the divine selection of a human leader. However, this exercise of divine authority is not unqualifiedly successful. *Success depends upon the subsequent actions of the human leader.*
>
> This portrayal, furthermore, suggests that the presence of God with the human leader or the leader's possession by the spirit of the Lord does not guarantee success. *Divine success appears contingent upon an appropriate human response.* Hence, the exercise of divine power is limited by the exercise of human freedom, the exercise of which frequently misuses and abuses human potential. Accordingly, the deity can influence but not command human actions; God will act to punish transgressions, but not to prevent them. (Bowman, 38–39; emphasis added)

Bowman's assessment is in keeping with what was suggested above concerning the decreasing effectiveness of the spirit of the LORD in the book of Judges, in terms of effecting deliverance. Whereas the first judge, Othniel, effected immediate deliverance when the "spirit of the LORD came upon him" (3:10), Gideon's possession by the spirit had comparatively little effect. To be sure, he swung into action; but he remained fearful and hesitant (6:33–40), and he ended up leading the people back into idolatry (8:22–28). Similarly, when "the spirit of the

LORD came upon Jephthah" (11:29), he made a foolish and unfaithful vow that led to the death of his daughter, an event followed by a bloody civil war (12:1–7). This trend is not encouraging. Not surprisingly, the spirit will come upon Samson *more* than upon any of the other judges, but with the *least* effect (see 14:6, 19; 15:14). To be sure, Samson's strength is impressive, and his feats are entertaining; but in terms of deliverance from oppression, which is God's purpose, they accomplish essentially nothing. In fact, Samson never even *attempts* to rally support for a general uprising against the Philistines.

In other words, Samson completely fails to demonstrate, in Bowman's terms, "an appropriate human response" to God's blessing and empowering him. Consequently, God's purpose remains unfulfilled. That Samson strikes even a passing blow at Philistine power—that he even *begins* to deliver Israel (v. 5)—is evidence not of his faithfulness but of God's persevering grace. If there's a faithful hero in the story, besides Samson's mother, it is the God who proves persistently faithful to Samson (see 16:28–31), who proves himself persistently unfaithful to God.

14:1—15:20 Lover Number One: The Woman from Timnah

It is revealing that Samson's first deed is falling in love with a Philistine woman, whom he orders his parents to "get . . . for me as my wife" (14:2). To this initial act of unfaithfulness on their son's part, Samson's parents object. In terms of the possible early origin of the story, their objection might have involved the requisite bride-price; but in terms of the final form of the book of Judges, to take a wife from among "the uncircumcised Philistines" (14:3) may be a violation of Samson's Nazirite status, which involves avoiding uncleanness. In any case, however, it is a violation of God's intent that the Israelites not collaborate with other peoples and nations (see 2:2; 3:6). Samson's response to his parents' objections shows that he *can be* persistent, at least when the matter involves sexual attraction rather than faithfulness. He repeats his order, "Get her for me" (14:3), accompanied by an explanation that NRSV translates, "because she pleases me." More literally, the explanation is this: "because she (is) right in my eyes" (see also 14:7). It is thus an ominous anticipation of the assessment that serves as an inclusio for the chaotic chapters 17—21: "all the people did what was right in their own eyes" (17:6; 21:25). As it turns out, Samson seems to have been an effective leader. Unfortunately, however, he will have led all the people in the wrong direction.

Thus, the next verse, 14:4, is all the more striking, as the narrator reports God's involvement in Samson's affair(s). The NRSV's "pretext" is misleading. God does not need "a pretext" to oppose Philistine oppression and injustice; God always opposes oppression. Rather, God needs "an opportunity" or "an occasion" (NIV), which God finds in the gifted but all-too-human Samson. In short, 14:4 is an affirmation that God works *incarnationally;* God works with the human resources at God's disposal, flawed as they may be in Samson's case, and indeed, in our own cases as well.

Judges 14:4 should not be understood as an affirmation of Samson's unfaithfulness and misbehavior. In a real sense, 14:4 finds a parallel in the frequently misunderstood Romans 8:28 and its affirmation "that all things work together for good for those who love God, who are called according to his purpose." This verse does not mean that everything we do is good or that everything turns out for the best. Rather, it means that God is able to redeem even our sinful selves and our worst misdeeds. So it will be with Samson. Even in the midst of his persistent self-assertion, Samson will be an instrument of God's purpose. A God who loves the world and who entrusts dominion to humankind (see Gen. 1:26–28) can work in no other way than incarnationally. This means that for love's sake, God risks that God's purpose will not be accomplished; and as suggested above, God's purpose is not fully accomplished by Samson. In other words, 14:4 must be heard in light of 13:5, and also in view of the larger context within and beyond the book of Judges.

That the reckless, oversexed, unfaithful Samson even *begins* to deliver Israel from the Philistines is testimony to God's faithfulness and persevering grace. In this respect, Samson's story is congruent with the entire biblical story, which is carried forward not by human faithfulness but by the faithfulness of God. For Samson, and for us, the good news is that God's grace abounds. Samson's story illustrates well the truth that the apostle Paul would later articulate—that we human instruments of God's purpose fulfill our vocations as "clay jars" (2 Cor. 4:7), demonstrating that our ministries are "by God's mercy" (2 Cor. 4:1). The further lesson that Paul articulates is particularly important for interpreting the Samson stories, since Samson has often been unambiguously construed as a mighty hero. As Paul puts it, "we have this treasure [that is, the revelation of Jesus that impels people to pursue God's purpose] in clay jars, so that it may be made clear that this extraordinary power belongs to God and does not come from us." In his better moments, Samson perceived this truth (see 15:18–20; 16:28–31); but most of Samson's deeds in chapters 14—16 are motivated by his pursuit of his own purposes rather than the purpose of God.

So, Samson gets his way, and makes his way to Timnah. The problem with Timnah is not only the attractive Philistine women, but also "the vineyards" (14:5), which presented a problem for Nazirites who were supposed to avoid anything having to do with wine and grapes (see Num. 6:1–4). Given the dangers lurking in Timnah, one might reasonably suppose that the roar of "a young lion" (14:5) may be God's way of addressing Samson to warn him to stay away (see Amos 1:2; 3:4, 8, where the roar of a lion signals God's word). If so, Samson doesn't get the message. He kills the lion. Granted, the "spirit of the LORD" apparently enables him to do this; but, given the ambiguity surrounding the spirit of the LORD in the book of Judges (see above), it is not clear that Samson has done the right thing. Why didn't he tell his parents? It may be that Nazirites were not supposed to come in contact with corpses (see Num. 6:6–8), and that Samson is aware that his parents take the Nazirite status, and God's purposes in general (see 14:3), far more seriously than he himself does. Then too, perhaps Samson doesn't want his parents to know that he has ignored a potential word from God. Or perhaps the narrator has Samson keep the information from his parents as part of a narrative strategy to build suspense (see 14:16).

Verse 7 reiterates that for Samson, the Timnite woman "(is) right in my eyes" (NRSV "she pleased Samson"; see 14:3). The return to the carcass of the lion (14:8) serves to set up Samson's riddle (14:8–14). Again, Samson makes contact with a dead body; and again, he does not tell his parents (14:9).

The "feast" (14:10) sponsored by Samson probably involves again his violation of his Nazirite status, since it is hard to imagine a seven-day party, then or now, without the presence of "wine and strong drink" (Num. 6:3), which a Nazirite was supposed to avoid. The riddling, counter-riddling, and revenge that take place at and after the feast gives the impression that perhaps everybody was just a bit under the influence of alcohol. But it is precisely at this point in the story that the categories of folklore studies become very helpful, as Samson is portrayed in the role of "trickster" (see above). Samson's riddle (14:11–14), for instance, which seems tacky and even rude in terms of contemporary etiquette, is part and parcel of the trickster motif.

Not only does Samson's proposal of the riddle seem rude, but the riddle itself seems inherently unfair. No one is in a position to answer this riddle except Samson himself, especially since he did not even tell his parents about the episode with the lion and later its carcass (see 14:6, 9). But, of course, the plot demands just such a riddle, in order to set up the Philistine's treachery in 14:15–18 and Samson's revenge in 15:19. Besides, such private-experience riddles are attested elsewhere in traditional stories from ancient cultures (see Crenshaw, 112–14). And, apparently, the Philistines readily expect this sort of strategy on Samson's part. They do, after all, solve the riddle!

To be sure, it does take them three days to figure out what Samson is up to (14:14). Presumably, in those three days, they conclude that the "obvious" answers to the riddle are not the ones Samson has in mind. The "obvious" answers that the Philistines wisely reject get into the bawdy humor of the story, something not new in the book of Judges (see Introduction, section 3e, and the commentary on 3:12–30; 5:1–31). Perhaps the most "obvious" answer to the riddle would be "vomit," and this answer would fit especially the context of a seven-day party, which in all likelihood would have featured an excess of food and drink. In such settings, "the eater" frequently indulges excessively, and so what goes into "the eater" comes back "out of the eater." Thus, "the strong" young partygoers throw up the delicacies—"something sweet"—they have consumed. The second "obvious" answer to the riddle also fits the context well. The party is to celebrate a wedding, and the second "obvious" answer involves sexual innuendo. In this case, "the eater" and "the strong" would be the groom; and "something to eat" and "something sweet" would be his semen, which the bride figuratively but pleasurably "consumes." While this possible answer may not be as obvious as the first, the riddle almost certainly contains this sexual innuendo, especially since eating is elsewhere a figure for sex (see Crenshaw, 114–17, where he cites Prov. 30:20).

In any case, the Philistines apparently conclude that these two possible answers are too obvious, so they go after Samson's wife, threatening to take her life if she does not manage to pry the answer out of Samson (14:15). She succeeds, in a feigned and persistent emotional display that anticipates Delilah's handling of Samson (see 16:15–17; note NRSV "nagged" in 14:17 and 16:16, although "pressed" would be a better translation; see NIV "continued to press" in 14:17). She then proceeds to give the solution to the Philistines, who answer Samson by asking questions (14:18), perhaps in an attempt to imply their superiority. The trickster has been tricked.

Before taking his revenge, another typical feature of trickster stories, Samson responds to the Philistines with an accusatory saying that, like the riddle, contains sexual innuendo (14:19). According to the narrator, "the spirit of the LORD" is involved in Samson's revenge (14:19); but as suggested above, it is revealing that Samson's killing of thirty Philistines accomplishes personal revenge, not the deliverance of his people. While the notice in 14:20 seems to bring this episode to a close, it actually amounts to another sort of trick on Samson that sets up another round of trickery and revenge.

When Samson discovers that his wife has been given to another (14:20—15:3), he is immediately intent upon revenge. While 15:3 suggests Samson's admission that his prior violent revenge had been hasty and blameworthy, it still does not prevent him from concluding that one bad turn deserves another. The stunt with the foxes and torches (15:4–5) is again impressive, but has nothing to do with the deliverance of the Israelites. Ironically, the wife who had previously lied to prevent being burned (see 14:15) is the victim of the Philistines' fiery counter-revenge (15:6). The cycle of revenge continues in 15:7–8 as Samson kills the perpetrators.

At this point, the story takes an unexpected twist. It is the Philistines' turn for revenge, which, according to form, they do seek (15:10). The surprise is that Samson is taken into custody by the men of Judah, who in turn hand him over to the Philistines (15:11–13). From their point of view (and from a historical point of view), this seems to be an expedient move. But, as suggested above, from the point of view of the book of Judges in its final form, this indicates that things have gotten about as bad as they can get. It is 15:11–13 that best explains why the pattern that characterizes the book of Judges is broken in chapters 13—16. The progressive deterioration that began with Gideon has now reached a point where the people do not even cry out for deliverance (see Introduction, section 2c). It never occurs to them that God, instead of the Philistines, might rule over them (15:11; see 8:22–23); for in essence the Israelites are in covenant, not with God, but with the Philistines (see 2:1–5). If the presence of the Philistines and other peoples in the land was "for the testing of Israel, to know whether Israel would obey the commandment of the LORD" (3:4), then the Israelites have *utterly failed!* They are completely acquiescent with Philistine rule. If an appropriate human response is needed for God to be able to deliver, as suggested above (see commentary on 13:1–25, especially the quotation from Richard Bowman), then it is no wonder that Samson can only *begin* to deliver Israel (13:5). To be sure, Samson himself proves none too faithful; but he may actually be more faithful than the Israelite people as a whole, with the apparent exception of Samson's parents, especially his mother (see commentary on 13:1–25).

Although betrayed by his own people, Samson takes it out on the Philistines in another act of revenge (15:14–17). Again "the spirit of the LORD" (v. 14) is involved, but again the revenge is personal, effecting no deliverance. The event recalls Shamgar's slaughter of six hundred Philistines (3:31). It is revealing that even though Shamgar is allotted only one verse, he is said to have "delivered Israel," something Samson cannot accomplish in four chapters. This is yet another subtle sign of the progressive deterioration that characterizes the book of Judges.

The episode of the Timnite women closes with a rare glimpse of Samson's faithfulness, anticipating as well the end of the episode with Delilah (see 16:28–31). Samson humbly attributes his victory to God, and he asks God for help—something the Israelites as a whole fail to do in chapters 13—16 (see above). Given Samson's persistent pursuit of his own purposes and his repeated violation of his Nazirite status in chapters 14—15, God's granting of Samson's request for water and life is an amazing display of grace. The episode recalls Exod. 17:1–7, God's provision of water from the rock to sustain unfaithful Israel in the wilderness. As Dennis Olson concludes, "The parallel with Israel's experience cements the identification of Samson not only as a judge but also as a metaphor for all Israel" (Olson, 851). To be sure, Samson's unfaithfulness is paralleled by Israel's unfaithfulness in the book of Judges, but beyond the book of Judges as well. Samson's story and Israel's story, here and throughout the canon and beyond (including the church's story in the New Testament and throughout the centuries up to now), are testimonies not to human faithfulness but to God's faithfulness. Therein lay Israel's hope; and we Christians profess, therein lies our hope, and indeed, the hope of the world.

16:1–3 Lover Number Two: The Woman of Whoredom at Gaza

As the second episode of the Samson stories begins, once again Samson is found in a place where no Nazirite, indeed no Israelite, ought to be—in the Philistine city of Gaza pursuing a Philistine woman, this time "a woman of whoredom" (NRSV "prostitute"). Considering the complications that accompanied his pursuit of the woman from Timnah (14:1—15:20), Samson apparently concludes that a prostitute will bring fewer entanglements. But given that Samson has already slaughtered numerous Philistines (see 14:19; 15:8, 15), destroyed their crops (15:5), and only recently (narratively speaking, at least) escaped from Philistine custody (15:14), safe sex in Philistine territory is out of the question.

While the Philistine woman occupies Samson, the Philistine men of Gaza are planning another trick. Figuring that Samson will be utterly exhausted after a night of physical exertion, the men of Gaza set up an ambush, expecting to capture Samson easily at daybreak. But, the trickster pattern is still operative (see above); and Samson outwits his opponents with a counter-trick. Samson comes earlier than expected, and not only does he escape the Philistines' trap, he also takes "the city gate" of Gaza with him (16:3). Quite literally, then, Samson does what else-where figuratively describes a military triumph—that is, he "possesses the gate of the enemy" (see Gen. 22:17; 24:60). But, quite tellingly, this is *not* a military victory, nor does Samson even attempt to use his tro-phy as a rallying point against the Philistines. For Samson himself, as much as for the people, deliverance seems to be out of the question.

Samson's escapades among the Philistines demonstrate again his unfaithfulness to his Nazirite status and to the divine will articulated earlier in the book of Judges (see 2:1–5; 3:4–6). Furthermore, although Samson outwits the men of Gaza, his decision to enter Philistine terri-tory again does not seem terribly bright. But, of course, the trickster motif demands this sort of plot. Samson's apparent lack of judgment is even more pronounced in the next episode; but at the same time, his culminating counter-trick is also more dramatic. As suggested above, the trickster pattern serves to represent the divine opposition to oppres-sion; and that God continues to use Samson, who is unfaithful and irres-olute (except perhaps in pursuing Philistine women), is testimony finally to a God who chooses to work incarnationally and whose strat-egy is grounded in grace (see commentary on 14:1—15:20; and see below, "Reflections: Samson and Culture Wars, Then and Now").

16:4–31 Lover Number Three: Delilah and Sam-son's Fatal Attraction

Samson never seems to learn. Despite at least two close calls in the previous episodes, and despite the inevitable complications that arise from his pursuit of Philistine women, Samson is at it again in 16:4. Fur-thermore, if Samson appeared somewhat naive about the dangers of Philistine sexual encounters in 16:1–3, here he appears utterly clueless. Delilah must have been incredibly attractive, because her tactics for obtaining information from Samson are not really very subtle. She quite directly asks Samson how he "could be bound, so that one could sub-due you" (16:6; see 16:5). Then she proceeds to bind Samson in accor-dance with the information he gave her, and she calls the Philistines (16:7–8). Samson escapes (16:9); but for someone who already knew the Philistines were out to get him, one round of this nonsense should have sufficed. But no! Delilah does the same thing again (16:10–12) and again (16:13–14)! Up to this point, Samson's apparent stupidity strains belief.

But there's more. Having apparently learned nothing from his dis-astrous experience with the woman from Timnah about the danger of

107

telling secrets (see 15:15–20), Samson falls prey to the same sort of feigned emotional appeal from Delilah (16:15–16; cf. 15:16–17). Ignoring also the three immediately preceding times that Delilah has summoned the waiting Philistines, Samson tells her the whole story—Nazirite status and all (16:17).

Samson's absolutely incredible stupidity has led to all sorts of speculation, psychoanalytic and otherwise—Samson's fascination with the forbidden, the lure of "the other," his compulsion to mix sex with danger, and so on. Alter, for instance, eloquently concludes: "The glint of the dagger in the velvet hand of love is what has excited him from Timnah onward" (Alter, 53). While such speculation is interesting, the plot of 16:4–31 tells us far more about the trickster pattern than it does about Samson's psychosexual dynamics. The plot virtually demands that Samson be tricked one final time by Delilah, in order to set up the requisite, but nonetheless dramatic, culminating counter-trick (See Matthews, "Freedom and Entrapment in the Samson Narrative," 253–57).

While the trickster pattern drives the unfolding plot, there are indications that the writer/editor has also introduced categories that Alter calls "psychological and moral" (Alter, 56). Alter points, for instance, to the fourfold repetition of the Hebrew root *p'm* in 16:15, 18, 20, 28 (NRSV "times," v. 15; "time," v. 18; "times," v. 20; and "once," v. 28). Interestingly, this root is also used rather distinctively in 13:25 to indicate that "the spirit of the LORD began to *stir* him." Alter construes the verb to connote a kind of drivenness or compulsion; and he sees Samson "in the grip of what psychoanalysis would call a repetition compulsion" (50), involving the linkage of sex and danger. This primarily psychological construal takes on a more pronounced moral dimension in chapter 16, however, where the repetition of "time(s)" in verses 15, 18, 20 highlights Samson's moral and even spiritual weakness. The progression of occurrences culminates in verse 28 when Samson finally looks to God, requesting renewed strength for just "this one time" (NRSV "this once").

This moral, or even theological, dimension is reinforced by the stated purpose of the gathering at which the captive Samson has been invited to provide the entertainment. The Philistines have "gathered to offer a great sacrifice to their god Dagon" (16:23), and to praise Dagon because he "'has given our enemy into our hand, the ravager of our country, who has killed many of us'" (16:24). From the narrator's perspective, of course, Dagon had nothing to do with Samson's misfortune. Rather, Samson virtually surrendered to the Philistines, falling into captivity because of his unfaithfulness to the Nazirite status, his unwillingness to be set apart as a servant of God's purpose rather than his own.

108

To be sure, the difference between the Philistine perspective and the narrator's/reader's perspective sharpens the moral, theological issues. The reader is reminded yet again that God cannot effect deliverance in the presence of unfaithful leaders and an unfaithful people. Although Samson has been set apart from birth and is apparently quite aware of his chosen status (see 16:17), his actions have been driven almost exclusively by the pursuit of his own purposes rather than God's purpose. The people have done no better. In Judges 13—16 they fail to cry out for help from God, and they even turn their once potential deliverer, Samson, over to the Philistines (15:9–13). Although God wills deliverance, there will be none in this story.

Even Samson's turn back to God is marked more by his desire for personal revenge against the Philistines than for deliverance for his people. In essence, Samson remains, to the very end, selfish, just as he remained until nearly the very end, clueless (see 16:20). That both Samson and the Israelites demonstrate such persistent unfaithfulness and self-assertion, thus thwarting God's purpose to deliver them from Philistine oppression, means that Judges 13—16 functions as a call to repentance, as does all the prophetic literature. In other words, it warns readers in every generation about the inevitably negative consequences of unfaithfulness and disobedience, including the injustice involved in ongoing oppression. Samson's turn back to God is too little, too late. He dies, although his work in the end can be taken at least as a *beginning* of Israel's deliverance (see 13:5). As for the people, they remain under Philistine domination; and in the remaining chapters of the book of Judges, the violence of external oppression will be accompanied by the tragedy of internal injustice and violence. The progressive deterioration that characterizes the book thus serves simultaneously as a warning about the results of idolatry and disobedience and as a call to repentance and faithfulness to God and God's purposes.

But if the conclusion to Samson's story sharpens its theological dimension, offering a word of warning, it also holds out a word of hope. From God's point of view, dealing with Samson and the Israelites must have been a monumentally frustrating endeavor. In terms of Samson specifically, what energy, strength, and talent have been squandered in trivial pursuits! So, for God to answer Samson's "deathbed" request "this one time" (v. 28) is an act of immeasurable patience, remarkable generosity, and amazing grace, as well as a demonstration of the effectiveness of a genuine turning to God and calling upon God's name. It bespeaks, in the face of persistent human unfaithfulness, the faithfulness of God. Samson repeatedly forgot God, as did the Israelites; but God will not forget Samson. In this case, the hopeful note is not that

109

God's purpose is fulfilled, because it is not. Rather, Israel's hope lies in the God who will be lovingly faithful to a ludicrously unfaithful people.

Reflections: Samson and Culture Wars, Then and Now

The preceding interpretation of Judges 13—16 differs significantly from the traditional presentation of Samson as a hero of faith, indeed, as a type of Christ. As pointed out, Samson is, almost without exception, faithless; and he fails to deliver his people. If there is a faithful hero in the story, it is God; and if there is a faithful human hero, it is Samson's mother. But if Judges 13—16 does not support the traditional construal of Samson, what is to be done with the stories of this "oversexed buffoon"?

Several interpretive directions have been suggested above. First, the stories of Samson are testimony to a God who works through human beings. Because God honors human integrity and freedom, God's purposes can be thwarted, as they are by both Samson and the people of Israel in Judges 13—16. That Samson even begins to deliver Israel is testimony to God's faithfulness amid the frustrations caused by a faithless leader and a faithless people. In short, Samson's story shows that God works by grace.

Second, the stories of Samson are testimony to a God who opposes oppression and who wills deliverance from it. What Samson fails to accomplish is the deliverance of the Israelites from cruel oppression. As scholars of folklore point out, a central message of the prevalent trickster pattern involves the struggle of the weak and marginalized against oppressive superior forces. Embedded in the hyperbole and humor of the trickster narratives about Samson is the theological conviction that the God of Israel wills life for all.

Taken together, these two testimonies are congruent with the portrayal of God throughout Scripture. Because humankind proves unfaithful from nearly the very beginning, according to the biblical story, God can only pursue God's fundamental purpose—justice that yields *shalom*, "peace"—by way of grace (see Introduction, section 4). In a world where millions, perhaps billions, of people remain poor, oppressed, and marginalized, this biblical testimony still cries out to be heard. In a world where hardly anyone believes in grace, this biblical testimony could hardly be more timely.

110

There is another major aspect of the trickster pattern in the Samson stories that also proves to be particularly pertinent. As suggested above, the trickster pattern overlaps with the portrayal of Samson as a hero of sorts—a "culture hero" rather than a hero of faith. In particular, Samson's Nazirite status has the effect of portraying him from birth as a sort of "extreme Israelite," one whose life is to be distinctively faithful to the God of Israel. In this sense, Samson should be a representative of God's will in the way that the narrator of the book of Judges describes from the beginning—faithful to God alone by avoiding contact with the people of the land (2:1–5; 3:1–6). In the list of people that God has left in the land to "test" the people's faithfulness, "the five lords of the Philistines" are mentioned first (3:3). The "test" in chapter 3 sets up a kind of "culture war," especially with the Philistines; and Samson, a Nazirite, should be a major combatant on God's side.

In a sense, of course, Samson is on God's side, insofar as he kills many Philistines. But, at the same time, Samson is constantly found in Philistine territory, especially in pursuit of Philistine women. To be sure, from one perspective this aspect of Samson's behavior can be understood as an Israelite means of affirming its equality with the supposedly superior Philistines—that is, our guy can compete for Philistine women with any of your own guys. But within the final form of the book of Judges and indeed the final form of chapters 13—16, Samson's Philistine-compulsion is terribly problematic; it bespeaks his unfaithfulness to his Nazirite status, as well as his unfaithfulness to the God of Israel and to God's purpose, which consequently is not accomplished. But it is precisely Samson's ambivalent behavior toward the Philistines that proves pertinent perhaps in helping the people of God in other times and places to assess their participation in culture wars.

How, for instance, can the church in North America participate in a culture that, in essence, teaches self-assertion (the central importance of the human self and its desires) and all but institutionalizes idolatry by encouraging people to believe that life consists in the abundance of possessions (see Luke 12:15)? This troubling question has, of course, occupied theologians throughout the twentieth century; and it still does. A prevalent and persuasive answer is that the church can and should be in the world but not of the world (see John 17:1–19, especially vv. 11, 14, 18). As H. Richard Niebuhr suggested, it is the mission of the church to transform culture (190–229). Or, in the words of Douglas John Hall, the church is called "To help God 'change the world'" (Hall, *Christian Mission*, 98).

This answer is undoubtedly biblical and faithful; and it is clearly related to the central issue throughout the book of Judges: Will Israel honor, trust, and obey God alone, amid the inhabitants of a new land and its gods? To proclaim and embody God's sovereign claim on our lives and the life of the whole world as our ultimate loyalty and allegiance will surely not only transform ourselves; it will also have, through us (see 2 Cor. 5:17–21, especially vv. 19–20), a transforming effect on the world. Through God's work in Christ and Christ's work in us, "there is a new creation" (2 Cor. 5:17). Jesus' disciples were known as "These people who have been turning the world upside down" (Acts 17:6). In short, they were transforming Greco-Roman culture; they were changing the world. That can and should be the mission of the church in every generation.

But the culture wars in Judges 13—16 serve to remind the people of God in every generation just how difficult a "test" (see 3:1, 4) it is to be faithful to God and God's purposes when living in a land that offers compelling, attractive alternatives. Samson exemplifies the difficulty. To be sure, he stands over against the Philistines, vehemently at times; but he is also apparently fascinated by their ways as well as by their women. Thus, Samson's behavior serves as a timely reminder to the people of God and their leaders in every generation of how easy it is to reflect the ways of a prevailing culture instead of transforming it, of how easy it is to become like the world rather than to change the world.

The people of God have always been tempted to reflect culture instead of transforming it, but perhaps the temptation is greater in North America today than at any other time or place in the history of God's people. The United States of America, for instance, is frequently characterized as "a Christian nation," as if to be a good citizen of the U.S.A. and a good Christian were identical. The prevalence of this notion makes it extremely difficult for the church to stand over against a culture that teaches the idolatry of self-sufficiency and that promotes greed as a virtue. In short, the church in the U.S.A. is sorely tested when it comes to transforming culture or changing the world.

Because this is so, in recent years theological voices have arisen to call the church, especially the church in the U.S.A., to a renewed awareness of its *alien* status—its *Nazirite* status, if you will, as a people set apart for God's purposes and not simply our own purposes or those of our culture or our nation. (See Stanley Hauerwas and William Willimon, *Resident Aliens: Life in the Christian Colony*, and Douglas John Hall, *The End of Christendom and the Future of Christianity*.) Not surprisingly, Hauerwas and Willimon criticize H. Richard Niebuhr, suggesting that his call for the church to transform culture was too optimistic, and that the church has heard Niebuhr's call as an invitation to take its agenda from the culture rather than from the gospel (see Hauerwas and Willimon, 39–43). Their criticism is perhaps somewhat unfair; but it at least serves as another reminder, alongside Judges 13—16, of how difficult it is to transform culture rather than merely reflect it. To be sure, Hauerwas and Willimon are not against transforming culture or changing the world. Rather, their point is that these things will happen only when the church attends first of all to being faithful to God and God's purposes. Changing the world begins with being a faithful church—by honoring, trusting, and obeying God alone (see Introduction, section 4). This is precisely the lesson that neither Samson nor the Israelites learned, but to which the book of Judges can call our attention.

The violence of the Samson narratives may also help us to appreciate that it really is a culture *war* in which we find ourselves. Hauerwas and Willimon too are aware of this, so they recommend renewed attention to a text like Ephesians 6:10–17, which enjoins the people of God to "take up the whole armor of God, so that you may be able to withstand on that evil day, and having done everything, to stand firm" (v. 13). The point, as Hauerwas and Willimon recognize, is not to glorify or commend violence in any way. Rather, the point is to remind the people of God that God's statement of purpose—the gospel—regularly *evokes* violent opposition. Witness what happened when Jesus announced the presence of the reign of God and invited people to enter it (see Mark 1:14–15). His announcement and embodiment of a new reality—a transformed culture, a changed world—landed him on a cross. The gospel still evokes opposition. Writer Flannery O'Connor once stated that people think the Christian faith is a security blanket. It's not, she said, it's a cross. When the people of God are faithful, in any time and place, they are in for a fight.

It is not coincidental in this regard that when Judges 3:1–6 portrays the Philistines and other people of the land as being "for the testing of Israel" (3:4), it also envisions that the Israelites will learn about "war" (vv. 1–2). The point is not that the Israelites will need to be aggressors, but rather that they will have to "withstand" and "stand firm" (Eph. 6:1, 3) against people like the Philistines and their ways. It is precisely this, of course, that Samson failed to do most of the time. Despite his Nazirite status, instead of withstanding Philistine ways, Samson embraced them, thus endangering his own life and failing to accomplish the deliverance that God willed. Thus, Samson's negative example can serve as a timely reminder of the seriousness of our culture wars, as well as a representation of the truth that to stand for God will mean to stand against idolatry, self-assertion, greed, and injustice. The real rub for citizens of the U.S.A. (and other nations as well) may be the discovery that to be a good citizen will mean to be a bad Christian.

To be sure, becoming a kind of Nazirite church, standing over against a deadly culture, may have its hazards as well. In their sequel to

113

Resident Aliens: Life in the Christian Colony, entitled *Where Resident Aliens Live,* Hauerwas and Willimon offer as a metaphor for Christian discipleship the experience of U.S. Marine Corps basic training at Parris Island (73–83). In this training (and remember, the word "disciple" means "student"), new Marines learn the rigors of a new way of life; they become, in essence, a "new creation" through the discipline offered them in the training. So far, so good, perhaps. The potential danger? These new Marines now despise the soft, permissive culture from which they came. To be sure, this may not be all bad; but the danger is that now they will *hate* the world, to which they have now become "superior." In fairness to Hauerwas and Willimon, it should be noted that they explicitly renounce any hatred toward the world (98). Unfortunately, however, the book of Judges has often been interpreted to mean that God hates the rest of the world beyond the Israelites— Philistines, Moabites, Ammonites, Midianites, Canaanites—and that so should God's people. But the point is not that God hates these other peoples and nations; rather, God has shown Israel a more excellent way—the way of faithfulness, obedience, justice, and peace—which they are called to embody and so to model for God's sake, for their own sake, and for the sake of the whole world (see Introduction, section 3).

In short, the culture wars in which the church always finds itself will be a struggle. There are dangers from either side. On the one side, the temptation is to acquiesce with the prevailing culture, as Samson and the Israelites usually did. On the other side, the temptation is to feel superior and even to hate those who are different, as interpreters of the book of Judges have often encouraged their hearers to do (and as, with or without the book of Judges, Christians have often done).

To be sure, Samson's story in Judges 13—16 offers no easy answers or clear-cut solutions to the contemporary people of God for their culture wars. Even so, Judges 13—16 performs the valuable service of calling the church's attention to the perennial issue of how faith and culture relate. In Susan Niditch's words again, "the tale of Samson is a powerful statement of hope and vindication as well as a visceral comment on problems inherent in relations with the non-Israelite world" ("Samson," 624). In particular, the behavior of Samson himself demonstrates how difficult it is to withstand the attractions of a prevailing culture, even a culture that is known to compromise clearly held convictions and that threatens death. What is certainly called for is constant vigilance as the church confronts contemporary culture, and almost certainly such vigilance will lead the church at least to begin to reject as a matter of faithfulness any residual advantages afforded it by a culture that is increasingly hostile to the gospel (see Placher, 161–83, especially

p. 178). A church largely enculturated, be it to the culture of North America or any other, is a church that, like Samson, will largely fail to be an agent of God's purpose.

One final aspect of Samson's Philistine enculturation deserves attention, because it has a decidedly modern ring—that is, his attraction to Philistine women. When people fail to be faithful to God, it always means that other gods get worshiped (see 2:3). In Samson's case, one of his gods seems to be an inordinate desire for sexual gratification; it so dominates the Samson stories as to be its most logical organizing principle (see above). It is this aspect of Samson's character that may remind us of contemporary politicians, but there is a more profound significance to the fact that sex for Samson becomes idolatrous. Not only do the stories of Samson remind us of the remarkable power of human sexuality, but they also illustrate the chaos that is produced when sexual gratification is not governed by faithfulness. Singer Joni Mitchell has a song entitled "Sex Kills," which could serve as an apt subtitle for Samson's career. Mitchell's point is not that sex is bad, but rather that human sexuality has become co-opted by advertisers to sell just about everything, and that sexuality is now all tied up with greed, injustice, and violence. In this sense, sex kills. For a contemporary culture that, like Samson, has turned sex into a god, Judges 13—16 is a warning about the destructive and deadly results of such idolatry and unfaithfulness. When sexuality ceases to be viewed as a good gift of God and becomes an ultimate concern, then for us, as much as for Samson, sex kills.

In the culture wars in which Samson and Israel were engaged, they were the big losers (along with God, perhaps, whose purpose is temporarily thwarted by Samson and the Israelites). For this reason, it is not surprising that the Samson narratives end without any mention of "rest" for the land. There is none; and indeed, there has been none since Judges 8:28. The progressive deterioration that began with Gideon has culminated with Samson, almost. Although Samson is the last and worst of the judges (at least within the book of Judges; see 1 Sam. 7:15—8:3), the situation of the people actually deteriorates further in chapters 17—21, to which we now turn.

PART THREE

Complete Deterioration and Terror

Judges 17:1—21:25

In these concluding chapters of the book of Judges, the life of the people of Israel falls completely apart. Because there are no more judges, chapters 17—21 are often viewed as an epilogue that derives from a later editor. But these chapters provide a nearly perfect conclusion to the book, in terms of the progressive deterioration that was anticipated in 1:1—2:5 and that has been occurring since Gideon. For here the deterioration is complete, and terror reigns on all sides. There is no external enemy, because the people are their own enemy. To be sure, there had been Israelite-on-Israelite violence in chapter 9 and in 12:1–7; but in chapters 17—21, the tribe of Benjamin is almost annihilated following the brutal killing of the Levite's concubine. Things could not get any worse (see Introduction, section 2c).

Samson's almost complete lack of concern for his Nazirite status and for God's purposes in general means that the Israelites have had an impressive model to teach them to do "what was right in their own eyes" (17:6). (See 14:3, where "pleases me" is literally "right in my own eyes," and 14:7 where "pleased Samson" is literally "right in the eyes of Samson.") This notice occurs again at 21:25, the last verse in the book, and thus serves as an inclusio for chapters 17—21. In both 17:6 and 21:25 it is preceded by the clause "In those days there was no king in Israel." This clause also occurs in 18:1 and 19:1, thus forming a refrain for the final chapters.

This linkage of the concluding chaos with the absence of kingship in Israel is often taken to mean that the book of Judges, or at least chapters 17—21, is a setup for the monarchy. More specifically, since chapters 19—21 reflect poorly on Gibeah, Saul's home, these chapters seem to offer ideological support for the future Davidic monarchy. These proposals make sense; but in the final form of the book of Judges, all Israel looks bad, including Judah. If the concluding chapters of the book of Judges are intended as a setup for the Davidic line or the

117

monarchy in general, it must also be remembered that the monarchy ended in chaos as well. The kings, as it turned out, also "did what was right in their own eyes." From this larger canonical perspective, chapters 17—21 do not offer ideological support for the monarchy; rather, they fit into the larger pattern of Israel's persistent unfaithfulness and disobedience. By depicting the horribly violent results of unfaithfulness and disobedience, chapters 17—21 function, as does all prophetic literature, both as a call to repentance and as an expression of hope in God's faithfulness to an unfaithful people.

What the people need to repent of, of course, is their unbridled self-assertion and idolatry, which have been a problem from the very beginning of the book of Judges, where the issue is whether the people will honor, trust, and obey God alone (see Introduction, sections 3 and 4, and the commentary on 1:1—2:5 and 2:6—3:6). From the beginning, too, self-assertion and idolatry have gone hand in hand, so it is not surprising that chapter 17 opens with the story of the making of an idol. That self-assertion and idolatry are the twin sins throughout the book is another sign of the unity of the book of Judges; that is, as suggested above, chapters 17—21 present the logical results of persistent idolatry and the prolonged failure to honor God's sovereignty.

So, again not surprisingly, the people who are weeping at the beginning of the book of Judges are weeping again at the end. The source of weeping at the beginning of the book is the people's unfaithfulness to the covenant, manifesting itself in idolatry (see 2:1–5). As the book of Judges has demonstrated all along the way, the people's unfaithfulness has produced violently chaotic results. The linkage of personal violence against the Levite's concubine (chap. 19) and the violent civil war that follows (chap. 20) is the tragic but logical culmination to the book of Judges. The violence involved in the civil war is the cause of the weeping at the end of the book (see 20:23, 26; 21:2). These two episodes of weeping provide a frame for the entire book of Judges. Along with the weeping at the center of the book (see 11:37–38 and the commentary on 11:29–40), they are another indication of the unity of the book of Judges, which is, as Tate suggests, "a book of weeping" (see commentary on 2:1–5).

An additional and related indication of the literary unity of the book of Judges is the noticeable anonymity in chapters 19—21 (see Don Michael Hudson). Whereas individual judges are featured in 3:7—16:31, the people are united in 1:1—3:6 and chapters 19—21. But the unity is ironic; for the people come together, in essence, to destroy Benjamin (see 20:1). This ironic twist is underscored by the lack of names in chapters 19—21, which as Hudson suggests, "gives the implicit impression that *every* individual was dangerous because every individual was doing right in his or her own eyes." The effect? "Anonymity as a literary device reflects the universality of violence and dismemberment" (Hudson, 60). Again, the literary form of the book of Judges invites the reader to construe the concluding chapters as the logical culmination of the preceding story of unfaithful self-assertion and idolatry.

That the final two blocks of material in the book of Judges are not simply random, unrelated appendages is further suggested by their similar patterns and the literary techniques they employ (see Philip Satterthwaite). For instance, both begin with stories of individual Israelites (chapters 17, 19) who become involved in tribal or multitribal situations (chaps. 18, 20—21). Also, both blocks of material clearly allude to other Old Testament material. In Judges 18, the movement of the Danites recalls major episodes in the earlier Israelite movement toward and settlement in the land (see especially Num. 13). Judges 19 recalls Genesis 19, and Judges 20 recalls the details of Joshua's capture of Ai (Josh. 8). But, as Satterthwaite concludes, "All these three allusions have a similar effect, that is, they suggest the theme of 'something going wrong in Israel'" (Satterthwaite, 85). Thus, not only do chapters 17—18 and chapters 19—21 cohere with each other; they also provide the continuation and indeed culmination of the downward spiral that began with Gideon and grew progressively worse with Jephthah and Samson. In short, chapters 17—21 are a logical, integral, and effective conclusion to the book of Judges.

Interestingly, Satterthwaite also suggests that Judges 17—21 is also an integral part of the larger unit, Joshua–Kings; and he even proposes that chapters 17—21 may have been written as an introduction to Samuel–Kings (p. 88). While this proposal inevitably remains speculative, it has the advantage of suggesting that Judges 17—21 is not simply a setup for monarchy in general or the Davidic line in particular. Rather, the kings of Israel and Judah will demonstrate the same faithless self-assertion and idolatry that is evident throughout the book of Judges, leading to the same results—injustice, violence, and chaos. By depicting the violently chaotic results of unfaithfulness and idolatry in a way that serves as both a fitting conclusion to the book of Judges and an appropriate introduction to the books of Samuel–Kings, Judges 17—21 proves to be a pivotal piece of prophetic literature (see Introduction, sections 3 and 4). It serves both as an indictment of the people's unfaithfulness and idolatry and as striking testimony to the God who has been and will remain faithful to a people who are so frustratingly faithless and incessantly idolatrous.

17:1—18:31
Micah, the Levite, and the Danites

Given the noticeable paucity of references to God's activity in chapters 17—21, especially chapters 17—18, it is interesting that the name "Micah" automatically poses the God question. It means, "Who is like Yah(weh)"? Given the content of chapters 17—18, however, the name "Micah" has a decidedly ironic ring; for it seems that absolutely *no one* in chapters 17—18 knows what God is like! Or, at least, no one has any idea of what God wills for God's people. Micah, for instance, is a thief, having stolen money from his own mother! To be sure, he has the decency to confess his sin and return the money (or did the curse his mother had uttered in Micah's hearing strike fear in Micah's heart?). But, at this point, the comedy of errors is just beginning.

That eleven hundred pieces of silver are involved is not a good sign. Delilah had betrayed Samson for eleven hundred pieces of silver (see 16:5). So, although there is no apparent intent to say that Delilah is Micah's mother (the text never says explicitly that Delilah was a Philistine!), the number itself does not bode well. Sure enough, even though Micah's mother says that the silver is to be consecrated "to the LORD" (17:3), it is to be used by Micah "to make an idol of cast metal." But Micah doesn't stop with the idol of cast metal; he also makes "an ephod and teraphim," thus recalling Gideon's turn for the worse (see 8:27 and the commentary on 8:22–35). And for bad measure, Micah establishes his own little priesthood, ordaining one of his sons to serve at his private shrine.

All of the above happens in only five verses, prompting the narrator's observation that "all the people did what was right in their own eyes" (17:6). Given that Micah and his mother have broken at least half of the Ten Commandments in only five verses, this observation is actually something of an understatement. They have created another god besides God; they have made an idol; they have used God's name wrongly; and Micah has stolen, thereby failing to honor his mother (and he may also have coveted along the way). In short, as has been the case from the beginning of the book of Judges, disobedience and idolatry go hand in hand. The unjust and violent consequences will be narrated in chapter 18.

Readers of the book of Judges and this commentary may object, pointing out that if the story of Micah originated prior to the monarchy (or purports to describe this era), and if (as is likely) the Ten Commandments were a later formulation, then it is unfair to hold Micah to this later standard. To be sure, from a purely historical perspective, there is some cogency to this objection; but, this objection fails to take seriously the shape of the canon. In the canonical sequence, the Israelites have been delivered from Egypt; they have been given the Torah (which is headed by the Ten Commandments); they have promised to be obedient to the Torah and loyal to God alone; after an initial round of disobedience and idolatry, they have been forgiven and given a renewed covenant (see Exod. 32—34); and Joshua and his successors, the judges, have been entrusted with enacting the covenant loyalty and obedience that God desires.

In *this canonical context*, Micah and his mother should have known better; and they should have done better. Indeed, in this canonical context, their behavior is nothing short of ludicrous. But, of course, this is precisely what the narrator wants to communicate. Because the behavior of Micah and his mother is so ludicrous, it provides a perfect culmination to the progressive deterioration that began with Gideon and continued with Jephthah and Samson. Or, as the narrator frames the final chapters, they provide a perfect illustration of what happens when people do "what was right in their own eyes" (17:6; see above, introduction to chaps. 17—21). Of course, Micah and his mother are not really the culmination of the progressive deterioration. Things will get even worse in chapters 19—21, but the story of Micah and his mother is not a bad way to start.

As suggested above, the narrator's intent is not simply to provide a setup for the monarchy, Davidic or otherwise, as the observation of "no king in Israel" (17:6) has often been interpreted. Again, the larger canonical context is crucial. The kings of Israel and Judah, including David (see especially 2 Sam. 11—12, where David also manages to break at least half of the Ten Commandments in a single episode), will also prove to be generally faithless and disobedient, doing what is "right in their own eyes" rather than in God's eyes. In this canonical context, Judges 17:1–6 functions (as does the whole book of Judges and the whole prophetic canon) as an indictment of unfaithfulness and idolatry, and as an invitation to renewed covenant loyalty—that is, to repentance.

The prophetic canon also regularly warns about and illustrates the disastrous effects of self-assertion and idolatry, and such will be the case as the narrative continues to unfold in the rest of chapter 17 and in chapter 18. A new character, the Levite from Bethlehem, is introduced in 17:7. Immediately, a new issue is raised: Why does this Levite have to go looking for a place to live? Historically speaking, the narrative may have originated before the service of the Levites was regularized (that

121

is, if a village could not support all of its Levites, then some had to leave to seek employment elsewhere). Or the narrative could be late; and it may reflect a time when Levites were put out of work, as it were, by the centralization of worship at the Temple in Jerusalem. In any case, in the current canonical context, it is very odd that we are presented with an itinerant Levite, who apparently is willing to sell his services to the highest bidder (or perhaps is just content to receive a bid!).

Needless to say, a system where religious functionaries sell their services, as the Levite does, is wide open for abuse. In fact, other prophetic books, including the book of Micah, warn about this very thing (see Hos. 4:4–10; Mic. 3:5–8, which, along with Judg. 17, may offer support for the centralization of the priesthood and worship in Josiah's time, as narrated in 2 Kgs. 23). The Levite becomes Micah's private priest (17:12), and Micah himself thinks his future is guaranteed as a result (17:13). Not surprisingly, neither situation will prevail, as chapter 18 will demonstrate. The Levite has been installed "in the house of Micah" (17:12) rather than in "the house of God" (18:31; see Amos 7:12–13). Again, this may reflect the early origin of this material, when teraphim were regularly kept in private households; but from the perspective of the final shape of the canon (with its Deuteronomistic, prophetic influence), such behavior is highly irregular. Indeed, it amounts to idolatry, the relegation of God to something other than first place. The violent and destructive events of chapter 18 reinforce this thoroughly prophetic message.

Chapter 18 begins with an abbreviated form of 17:6. Even though it is not explicitly stated that "all the people did what was right in their own eyes," the no-king formula is sufficient to communicate this conclusion; and the content of the chapter bears this out. The Danites' behavior in the story clearly illustrates that the operative principle is not God's will, but rather the dictum that "might makes right."

The movement of the Danites in chapter 18 reflects the tradition that the Danites did not end up in the place originally allotted to them (see Josh. 19:40–48). Actually, Judges 18:1 seems to contradict Joshua 19:40–48, which suggests that the Danites were originally given an allotment that they subsequently lost. In either case, the Danites in Judges 18 are looking for a home. As suggested above, the way they proceed recalls the way Israel as a whole had moved toward settlement in the land. The most explicit recalling of earlier material involves the Danites' sending of spies into the land (see Numbers 13). The spies happen upon Micah's house, where they recognize the Levite, who happily admits that he is a priest-for-hire (18:2–5; see commentary on vv. 19–20). The Danites, not surprisingly given their subsequent behavior,

122

have no problem with this; and they seek and obtain a priestly blessing, which promises them success (18:6).

This blessing might seem to legitimate the Danites' subsequent behavior, but consider the source! The blessing comes not from "the house of God" (18:31), but rather from the house of Micah and from Micah's private priest-for-hire. Indeed, verse 6 anticipates verses 19–20, where it becomes eminently clear that the Levite is an idolatrous priest whose sole authorization is how much money one is willing to pay. The only thing that authorizes the Danites' behavior in Judges 18 is the fact that they are strong enough to get away with doing what is right in their own eyes (see vv. 25–26). Again, the operative principle is, "Might makes right."

Although the use of spies recalls Numbers 13, the report of the spies in Judges 18 differs significantly. Whereas the spies in Numbers 13 had encountered intimidating giants, the spies in Judges 18 suggest that the inhabitants of Laish are a pushover. The effect of the report in Numbers 13 is to affirm the people's need for God's help against a superior opponent. There is no such need in Judges 18; and this difference is in keeping with the Danites' orientation throughout the story. Although the spies claim God's support (v. 10), there is absolutely no warrant for this claim, except the blessing of a bogus priest. But, as the context makes clear, the Danites are doing nothing other than what is right in their own eyes. They could not care less about God, God's will, or God's help.

So, the Danites end up murdering the people of Laish, who are twice identified as "quiet and unsuspecting" (18:7, 27; see also "unsuspecting" in v. 10, as well as "securely" in v. 7, which is from the same Hebrew root). The fourfold repetition of the Hebrew root translated "unsuspecting"/"securely" is interesting, because its more literal translation points out precisely what the Danites lack. The root more literally means "trust." To be sure, the object of the people's trust is not specified; however, the prominent use of this important Old Testament root reminds the readers that the Danites are *not* a trusting or trustworthy people. At least, they have no trust in God, as God's people are supposed to have. If anything, they trust only themselves. In short, they are a perfect paradigm of what it means to do right in one's own eyes.

The horror of the Danites' slaughter of the people of Laish is further underscored by the repetition of "quiet" (18:7, 27). This word represents the same Hebrew word translated as "rest" in Judges 3:11, 30; 5:31; 8:27. In these earlier occurrences in the book of Judges, "rest" indicates very positively what God wills for a people. Thus, as well as anyone in the book of Judges, the people of Laish embody what God

123

intends. The irony of all this is that the name "Dan" is similar to a Hebrew word that means "justice." The Danites could hardly be further from the justice that God wills among all peoples and nations (see Introduction, section 4).

Two more aspects of chapter 18 indicate clearly the utter inappropriateness of the Danites' behavior. First is the way that the Danites treat Micah. Prior to their slaughter of the people of Laish, the Danites have already revealed their true character by, in essence, plundering Micah and his household, stealing his idol, ephod, teraphim, and priest (18:14–20). To be sure, it is difficult to have much sympathy for either Micah or the Levite, given their behavior earlier in the story; but this is precisely part of the point. *Everybody* in the story looks bad, because the people are all doing what is right in their own eyes. But the Danites look the worst. When the injustice of their actions is pointed out by Micah (18:24), all the Danites can reply is, in effect: "Shut up, or we'll kill you." Verse 26 summarizes the situation: "Might makes right." And, of course, this will inevitably and always be the case when people are doing what is right in their own eyes, rather than honoring God's sovereign claim.

The second aspect of chapter 18 that indicates the utter inappropriateness of the Danites' behavior is related to the first—namely, their explicit idolatry. The Danites have stolen Micah's idol. Theoretically, they could have melted it down for silver. But instead, they maintain Micah's idolatrous worship (18:30–31). Thus, the idolatry of one man has become the idolatry of an entire tribe (a tribe that, according to Josh. 24:18, 21, 24, has promised to worship/serve and obey God alone). What is more, according to v. 30, Moses' grandson and great-grandsons serve as the Danites' priesthood. What could be more ludicrous than the descendants of Moses presiding over an overtly idolatrous cult?

The reference to Moses in 18:30–31 is also a further reminder that the movement of the Danites has, in some sense, paralleled the earlier movement of the people as a whole toward the land of Canaan. Satterthwaite summarizes the character and effect of the parallels between Judges 18 and the books of Exodus, Numbers, and Joshua:

> There are a number of elements common to the two accounts: the sending of spies; the mustering of fighting men; the named places where the Danites camped along the way; the capture and renaming of a non-Israelite city at the end. But everything about this exodus and conquest is wrong: the Danites are unscrupulous plunderers, their cult is corrupt, and they destroy an innocent people. (Satterthwaite, 84)

Indeed, things are so wrong in Judges 18, and the Danites' behavior is so repulsive, that it is hard not to conclude that Judges 18 is an intentional polemic against Dan, probably because Dan and Bethel became the two northern cultic sites that rivaled Jerusalem. (See Yairah Amit, "Hidden Polemic in the Conquest of Dan." Amit also finds a "hidden polemic" against Bethel in Judges 17, concluding that the name "Ephraim" is meant to communicate "Bethel.") But, if Judges 17—18 ever were intended to advocate the claims of the Davidic dynasty and its connection to Jerusalem, its *present context* does not allow its function to be so limited.

Rather, the formula in 17:6 and 18:1, as well as in 19:1 and 21:25, presents the activity in Judges 17—18 as evidence that the people as a whole had gone wrong. This is all the more so because the progressive deterioration that began with Gideon finds its culmination in Judges 17—21. Although the primary actors in Judges 17—18 are representative of the eventual northern kingdom (that is, Ephraim and Dan), this will not be the case in Judges 19—21, where all the tribes, including Judah, are drawn into the bloody mess. If chapters 17—18 leave any question, chapters 19—21 will make it abundantly clear that everything and everybody have gone desperately wrong.

19:1—21:25
A Battered Woman and a Brutal War

Just when it seemed that things could not get any worse, they do. The story of the Levite and his concubine in Judges 19 is another of Phyllis Trible's "texts of terror" (see commentary on Judg. 11:29–40). As if the details of this story were not horrible enough, the aftermath of the rape and murder of the Levite's concubine involves a bloody civil war in which the tribe of Benjamin is nearly annihilated; and the misguided attempt to address this tragedy leads to the additional rapes of six hundred women. At this point, things truly *cannot* get any worse; and the book of Judges ends.

The rape of the Levite's concubine and the subsequent unraveling of any semblance of decency and order among the Israelites are integrally related (Keefe). Scenes of rape in Judges 19 and 21 frame this concluding section of the book of Judges. This literary arrangement highlights their significance, which Keefe summarizes as follows:

125

These rape scenes are embedded within a gendered symbol system in which male authority is entrusted with control. But the system does not leave the feminine wholly disempowered or marginalized. The wars of men fall subject to critique and judgment through these tales of rape and the horror that is known through the eyes of these violated women. Woman's body as a sign for community, connectedness, and covenant in these Hebrew narratives offers, through images of victimization and violation, powerful rhetorical figures of witness against the realities of brokenness within the human community. (Keefe, 94)

Keefe's conclusions provide a helpful perspective on the other framing device in Judges 19—21—that is, the repetition of the no-king formula in 19:1 and 21:25. The latter instance also contains the observation that "all the people did what was right in their own eyes," thus serving as part of a framing device for the larger unit, Judges 17—21 (see 17:6; 18:1). Because stories of the abuse of women serve to pass judgment on male-dominated institutions, the no-king formula in 19:1 and 21:25 cannot be construed as simply a setup for the monarchy, Davidic or otherwise. Especially when Judges 19—21 and the entire book of Judges is heard in its larger canonical context, readers will know that the male-dominated institution of kingship failed as miserably as did the office of judge.

From this larger canonical perspective, the book of Judges, like all the books in the prophetic canon, is a powerful witness against any institution—including the monarchy—that fosters idolatry and disobedience and thus contributes to the injustice and brokenness of the human community. The terrifying stories of brokenness in Judges 19—21 demonstrate graphically what happens when people are bent upon self-assertion and idolatry rather than submission to God and God's purposes. As such, they are a fitting and forceful conclusion to the book of Judges, in which the people of God have been self-assertive and idolatrous from the beginning (see commentary on 1:1—2:5). Furthermore, from Gideon onward, the judges themselves have increasingly exemplified the self-assertion and idolatrous ways that Israel was supposed to avoid. This spiral of progressive deterioration reaches its nadir in Judges 19—21. Things cannot get any worse. By documenting the terrifying effects of self-assertion and idolatry, these chapters, like the book of Judges as a whole, call people in every age to repentance; and they point them to a more excellent way—the way of covenant loyalty that finds expression in the pursuit of justice and righteousness. It is loyalty to God and God's ways that yields peace and life rather than hostility, abuse, violence, and death.

126   To be sure, Judges 19—21 anticipate the monarchy, in that the monarchy was explicitly entrusted with the embodiment of God's justice and righteousness (see 1 Sam. 8; 1 Kgs. 8; Ps. 72:1–7, 12–14; Jer.

22:13–17), and in that the subsequent narratives in 1 Samuel narrate the rise of the monarchy. But the failure of the monarchy illustrates that the essence of God's will involves not the perpetration of any particular political structure, but rather the establishment of justice and righteousness. By showing how tragic and violent is the failure to honor God and embody God's purposes, Judges 19—21 call people in every time and place to set self-centeredness aside, to embrace God's purpose for the world, and so to contribute to the wholeness of the human community—a condition that may be summarized by the words "justice" and "righteousness." Although the judges, or "bringers of justice" (see Introduction, section 2a), may have failed; and although the kings would fail as well; God did not give up and has not given up on God's purposes for the world. From the Christian perspective, there would one day be a king in Israel, Jesus of Nazareth, who would truly embody justice and righteousness, and who would gather a people to be devoted to loving the world as God loves the world.

But, of course, the Christian church has no reason to boast. Unfortunately, church history is full of stories that often make it read like a "text of terror"—the marginalization and abuse of women, as in Judges 19, and violent self-assertion that the church has often attempted to cloak in religious garb, as in Judges 20—21. And yet, like all the prophetic books, not only does the book of Judges warn and call to repentance, but it also offers hope. To be sure, the hope resides not in the possibility that Israel or the church will finally get things right. Israel seldom did, and the church seldom has. Rather, the hope lies in the God who, even after God's people have proven abysmally faithless and unjust, is not willing to let this people go. When the book of Judges is heard in its canonical setting, the good news is that even when things cannot get any worse, the story is not over. God will try again and again to reach and to use a frustratingly faithless and inveterately disobedient people for God's purposes; and God is trying still. The one word that best describes this divine attempt is *grace* (see Introduction, section 4).

19:1–30 Terror Reigns: The Levite and His Concubine

Chapter 19 begins exactly the way chapter 18 did (see also 17:6; 21:25; and the commentary above). Given the terrible things that happen in chapter 18, the reader expects that chapter 19 will be no different. Like chapter 17, chapter 19 features an unnamed Levite, and this does not bode well either. And sure enough, chapter 19 will reveal Israel at its very worst. Despite these negative clues at the beginning, however, the action actually begins with what sounds like a promising note—that is, an estranged couple seem on the verge of being reunited (19:3).

There are several puzzling features in chapter 19. The first involves a textual variant in verse 2 (see NRSV note: "prostituted herself against"). The NRSV has chosen to follow the Greek translation ("became angry with"). This reading may appear to make the concubine unusually assertive, but women with initiative are nothing new in the book of Judges (see 1:11–15; 4:1—5:31; 11:37–40). If the Hebrew text is the original, it is difficult to understand why the Levite would go after the concubine, except to punish her; but verse 3 gives every indication that he really wanted her back, enough to "speak tenderly to her," which is the language of love. In any case, the Levite goes to the father's house, to which the concubine has fled. Here he is welcomed warmly by the woman's father. Of the concubine's response we learn nothing. Nor shall we really learn anything about her throughout the story; she remains nameless and silent.

The nature of the social dynamics at the father's house is another puzzling feature of Judges 19 (vv. 4–9). Just exactly what is going on here? The father's hospitality seems comically exaggerated, but why? Are the five days of eating and drinking a case of male bonding, as several scholars suggest, the effect of which is to emphasize the marginalization of the concubine? Or does the father seek to detain the Levite as long as possible, because he fears for his daughter's safety and wants to keep her in his household as long as possible? Or, is the exaggerated hospitality some kind of power play between the father and the husband, not male bonding but competition between the males for the claim on the daughter/concubine? There seems to be no definitive answer to these questions; however, in any case, it is evident that the concubine herself has been relegated to the role of object rather than the active subject that she was in v. 2—a not unusual situation when men are bargaining and when male honor is at stake. (On the dynamics between the Levite and his father-in-law, see Victor H. Matthews, "Hospitality and Hostility in Genesis 19 and Judges 19," 6–7.)

Given this movement in the narrative, it is not surprising that, when the Levite finally manages to tear himself away from the father's hospitality, the presence of his concubine is noted almost as an afterthought (v. 10). Even the donkeys are mentioned before she is! If, as scholars have often suggested, chapters 17—21 are pro-Davidic material, it is striking that Jebus/Jerusalem is bypassed because it is "a city of foreigners" (v. 12; but, of course, this does have the effect of making Gibeah, the home of Saul, look all the worse). To be sure, this may well reflect the historical realities of the premonarchic period (see also 1:21; but compare 1:8). In any case, the bypassing of Jerusalem sets up the tragic irony that is to follow. Gibeah, the place that is supposed to be safe, will be the site of horrible inhospitality and violence.

The first sign that something is terribly wrong is that the Levite and his party reach the town square of Gibeah, and "no one took them in to spend the night" (v. 15). The custom of hospitality was characteristic of the ancient Near East; and in Israel, it was a matter of covenant loyalty to God to extend hospitality to strangers (see Exod. 22:21; 23:9; Lev. 19:33–34; Deut. 16:14; 26:12), in keeping with the divine hospitality Israel had received when it was a stranger (Deut. 10:18–19). Included among those who were to receive special care were the Levites, who had received no inheritance of land (see Deut. 16:14; 26:12). But in Judges 19, the stranger in Gibeah is also a Levite; and he is completely ignored by the people of the city.

This state of affairs is another graphic indication that the people of Israel were doing "what was right in their own eyes" (17:6; 21:25). So as to emphasize that the people of Gibeah are Israelites and thus should have known and done much better, the narrator twice reports the Benjaminite identity of Gibeah (vv. 14, 16). An additional irony in the story is that the Levites were the ones entrusted in Israel with teaching the provisions of the covenant (see Deut. 31:12). As Olson puts it, "If Gibeah is any sign of what is typical in Israel, the Levites have failed miserably as teachers of the law in regard to hospitality" (Olson, 876).

Of course, chapters 17—18 have shown that the Levites were failing miserably in several ways. The Levite in chapters 17—18 set up an idolatrous shrine, and he sold his services to the highest bidder. And, as chapters 19—21 unfold, the Levite here does not exactly appear in a flattering light. Although he seemed to start out on the right foot by seeking a reconciliation with the estranged concubine (v. 3), he subsequently ignores her, at best; and at worst, he is an accomplice to her murder. And his motive for seeking revenge against Benjamin on account of Gibeah's crimes seems to have more to do with his own status than it does with any concern for the murdered concubine (see below). In short, the portrayal of the Levite is hardly more positive than the portrayal of the people of Gibeah. Again, the point is clear—everybody was doing "what was right in their own eyes" (17:6; 21:25).

Well, almost everybody. Actually, there is one faithful and decent character in chapter 19 (besides the victimized concubine). It is the old man, who takes the Levite and his party into his home and proceeds to care for their every need (vv. 20–21). But of course, this old man is himself a stranger or sojourner in Gibeah (v. 16), so his actions serve to throw into even sharper relief the inhospitality of the people of Gibeah. The Levite and his concubine will have anything but the "Peace" wished them by the old man (see Matthews, "Hospitality and Hostility," 7–11).

If their ignoring of the Levite and his party was the first sign of their inhospitality, it pales in comparison to what the people of Gibeah do next. The men of Gibeah (or at least an undesirable element of the male population, which goes unhindered by the larger populace) move rapidly from inhospitality to sheer brutality. Their desire to have intercourse with the Levite is not primarily a matter of homosexuality, but of hospitality, or rather, inhospitality. The men of Gibeah intend to demonstrate their complete superiority over the Levite by subjecting him to what amounted in their culture to utter humiliation. Why they want to do this is not clear, except to say that their behavior is a graphic illustration of the violence that ultimately happens when people pursue what is "right in their own eyes." Indeed, this framing device for chapters 17—21 (see 17:6; 21:25) is echoed in what the old man says to the men of Gibeah when he offers them his virgin daughter and the Levite's concubine: "do whatever you want to them," or more literally, "do to them what is good *in your own eyes*" (v. 24). And they did.

The behavior of the men of Gibeah obviously recalls Genesis 19 and the behavior of the men of Sodom. In Genesis 19 as well, the issue is not homosexuality, but rather inhospitality (see Ezek. 16:48–49). Obviously too, in both Genesis 19 and Judges 19, the brunt of the mistreatment falls upon women. There is no question that both texts reflect a patriarchal culture in which the customs of hospitality favored males. In Judges 19 the old man that hosts the Levite and his party recognizes that it would be a greater breach of hospitality for the men of Gibeah to rape the Levite than it would be for them to rape his own daughter and the Levite's concubine. So, in accordance with prevailing customs, he offers the two women to the men of Gibeah.

This is not to say that the prevailing customs of the day would not have viewed the behavior of the men of Gibeah as an outrage. While the mistreatment of women may have been the lesser of the evils, according to prevailing custom, it would still have been viewed as an act of terror. The whole context of Judges 17—21 presents the actions of the men of Gibeah as a worst-case scenario—that is, an example of how horrible things are when people act out of self-assertion rather than divine direction. When human beings do what is right in their own eyes, the inevitable result is violent chaos.

The horror of the scene involves not just the rape of the concubine by the men of Gibeah, but also the treatment accorded her by her husband. Apparently, the Levite doesn't even stay awake to see what happens. Perhaps this isn't so surprising after all, however, since the Levite is the one who had handed her over to the men of Gibeah (v. 25). In any case, the Levite clearly makes no attempt to help nor does he seem to care at all about the treatment the woman has received. Rather, after waking in the morning and apparently getting ready to leave, the Levite virtually trips over the concubine, who lies prostrate in the doorway. Things could not be worse! The Levite does not even know whether his wife is dead or alive, and neither does the reader. The lack of a response from the concubine implies that she is dead, but the uncertainty in the Hebrew text only increases the horror.

Dead or alive, the woman is apparently hoisted onto a donkey like a sack of wheat. The text offers not the least hint of emotion on the part of the Levite. "The Levite is totally self-absorbed, unremorseful, and unfeeling" (Olson, 877). In short, the men of Gibeah are not the only ones who are doing right in their own eyes. So are the Levites, at least this Levite, who above all should have known better and done better (see above; see also the commentary on chapters 17—18).

That the woman is put on a donkey recalls Judges 1:14, where the woman Achsah is also riding on a donkey. The two scenes form a tragic envelope-structure for the book of Judges. Whereas Achsah is an active subject, stating her desire for "a present" or "a blessing" from her father, and getting it, the Levite's concubine remains nameless and without a voice. Whereas Achsah prospers, the Levite's concubine is tragically victimized. This envelope-structure is part of the larger pattern in the book of Judges. The progressive deterioration that starts with Gideon and reaches its nadir in Judges 17—21 is signaled in part by the increasing violence against women (see Introduction, sections 2c and 3d). It is the case, then and now, that the disease of a society manifests itself in the abuse of women.

Indeed, as Keefe points out (see above), violence against women serves to communicate in the Old Testament the degradation and disarray of the larger social structure. In Genesis 34 and 2 Samuel 13 as well as in Judges 19—21, the Hebrew verb *'nh* (NRSV "ravish" in Judg. 19:24 and "raped" in Judg. 20:5) occurs along with the Hebrew word *něbālāh* (NRSV "vile thing" in Judg. 19:24 and "vile outrage" in Judg. 20:6). In all three texts, the rape of a woman—Dinah in Genesis 34, the Levite's concubine in Judges 19, and Tamar in 2 Samuel 13—points to the unraveling of the larger social fabric. As Keefe puts it:

> The cry against rape as *něbālāh* points to an understanding in which the gravity of the crime is measured not primarily in terms of the consequences for the individuals involved, either victim or rapist, but as

131

> [a] disruption of and a violation against the order of community life.
> (Keefe, 82)

The whole point of Judges 17—21 is that Israelite community life has *completely* deteriorated. Everyone, men of Gibeah and Levite alike, are doing right in their own eyes. The only possible result is the kind of horrible violence narrated in Judges 19.

Lest the contemporary reader be tempted to feel superior or dismiss the Bible as a violent book, it is essential that we "recognize the contemporaneity of the story" (Trible, 87). The problem is not just that the ancient Israelites were self-assertive and violent, but rather the problem is also that *we* are self-assertive and violent. Violence against and abuse of women is at least as much a present reality as it was an ancient reality. According to Trible, Judges 19 finally calls us to repentance. In so doing, it functions like the whole book of Judges and the entire prophetic canon. By describing as clearly and graphically as possible the horrible, terror-filled, violent consequences of human self-assertion and idolatry—that is, everybody doing what is right in their own eyes—Judges 19, the book of Judges, and the prophetic canon invite repentance and conformity of self and society to the just, righteous, and peaceful purposes of God.

In what she labels her "Critique of Phyllis Trible's Interpretation" from a womanist perspective, Koala Jones-Warsaw suggests that Trible's perspective is too narrow. Reducing the social dynamics in Judges 19 to males victimizing females is problematic, because this dichotomy is itself a patriarchal way of thinking. As Jones-Warsaw concludes:

> It seems that Trible reduces this story to the victimization of women—which does not adequately account for the complexity of the problems in that society. It was a society in chaos. By reducing the problem of victimization to gender, she victimizes the other characters with a silencing technique comparable to that used by the narrator. (Jones-Warsaw, 28–29)

The advantage of Jones-Warsaw's approach is that she carefully maintains the connection between chapter 19 and chapters 20—21. To be sure, women are victimized in these chapters—the Levite's concubine and later the young women of Jabesh-gilead and Shiloh (21:8–24)—but there are many more victims as well. Because Israel was indeed "a society in chaos," the whole tribe of Benjamin is nearly wiped out (chap. 20), as is the population of Jabesh-gilead, except for the four hundred young women needed as wives for the surviving male Benjaminites (see 21:8–12). This whole violent fiasco produced plenty of victims; and in essence, this is the real point. In a society where people pursue their own self-interest rather than the purposes of God, *everybody* eventually stands to lose.

The narrative connection between chapter 19 and chapters 20—21 is evident in 19:29–30. Jones-Warsaw puts the best possible light on the Levite's course of action in vv. 29–30, suggesting that it shows the Levite has "changed the ordeal from a personal matter to a community matter" (25). This does seem to be the case; however, the Levite's dismembering of the concubine's corpse also seems unnecessarily brutal. This impression is intensified when the Levite's action is read in the light of Saul's dismemberment of oxen in 1 Samuel 11:6–11 in order to summon the Israelite tribes. Not only is Saul's action less grotesque, but it also serves the constructive purpose of leading to the deliverance of Jabesh-gilead. Judges 19 seems to be an intentional parody of 1 Samuel 11:6–11 with the object of communicating "the perversity of the events described in Judges 19—21" (Lasine, 43). In short, the Levite's brutal action has no redeeming social value. The Levite has no more concern for his murdered wife than he did while she was being raped and killed. Indeed, the Levite's motive for summoning "all the Israelites" (v. 30) may well be that he feels that *he* has been insulted. In his mind, the real outrage is that he has been denied hospitality and thus dishonored by the men of Gibeah, not that the concubine has been killed. If this is the case, then the Levite's consistent self-absorption is further evidence that Israel is a society in chaos. In any case, the brutal invitation extended in 19:29–30 leads directly into the events of chapters 20—21.

20:1—21:25 Civil War: From the Victimization of One to the Victimization of Many

In response to the Levite's gruesome invitation, "all the Israelites . . . assembled in one body before the LORD at Mizpah" (20:1). The narrator is careful to emphasize the inclusivity and unity of the gathering. The word "all" occurs five times in 20:1–11 (vv. 1, 2, 7, 8, 11; see also 19:30), and along with the word "one" (vv. 1, 11), it forms an envelope structure for 20:1–11. But the irony is overwhelming. Thinking that they have gathered to "purge the evil from Israel" (20:13), the gathered people are actually poised to annihilate their brothers and sisters. To be sure, they eventually realize their mistake (see 21:2–3, 13–15); but it's a matter of too little, too late. The horrible damage has been done (see 20:48); and apparently operating on the assumption that two wrongs do make a right, the Israelites slip further into the abyss of their terrifying

133

folly when they seek wives for the six hundred surviving Benjaminites (see 21:8–24).

The whole sordid story belies the claim that the people were actually gathered "before the LORD" (20:1). Rather, as the framing structure of chapters 17—21 suggest (17:6; 21:25; see also 18:1, 19:1), all the action in chapters 20—21 continues to take place under the rubric of everyone doing "what was right in their own eyes." Thus, later in chapter 20 when the text relates that the people "inquired of God" (v. 18) or "inquired of the LORD" (vv. 23, 27), the reader cannot help but be suspicious. In other words, the larger literary setting of chapter 20 subverts the claims of vv. 18, 23, 27. There is every appearance that, although the people may have thought they were inquiring of the LORD, they are actually seeking to give divine sanction to the battle plans that they *had already made on their own* in verses 1–17. The reader is made doubly suspicious by the fact that the LORD is reported to have been correct only one out of three times!

The first inquiry in v. 18 is particularly haunting. The question that the people put to God recalls Judges 1:1, and God's response in v. 18 is nearly identical to Judges 1:2: "Judah shall go up." But in this case, of course, Judah is to go up *against its own brothers and sisters!* No longer are the Canaanites the enemy. The people are their own worst enemy, persisting as they do in idolatry and self-assertion. Initial suspicion has already been raised in the mind of the reader by the way the Levite recounts what happened in Gibeah. To be sure, as Jones-Warsaw suggests (see above), the Levite correctly realizes that the crime committed at Gibeah is a community matter, not just a personal one. The Levite's motives, however, are suspect. He seems to be more upset about having been personally insulted than he is about his wife's death. Plus, he conveniently omits his own complicity in the crime (see 19:25); and his sense of outrage seems terribly exaggerated, given his own unwillingness to help his concubine and his own lack of concern about her well-being.

To be sure, as the Levite says, "a vile outrage" (20:6) has been committed (see above on *nĕbālāh*). But neither he nor the assembled Israelites demonstrate any sense of proportion in response to this crime. According to the Torah, punishment should be proportional to the crime—"eye for eye, tooth for tooth" (Exod. 21:24), meaning *no more than* an eye for an eye, and a tooth for a tooth. Thus, while retribution is permitted, it is to be limited. In Judges 20, however, this sense of limitation is sadly lacking. Not only do the assembled Israelites go after Benjamin without divine support (see above), but they also refuse to stop the attack until they have nearly wiped out the whole tribe.

Again, the irony is staggering. The Israelites don't stop with destroying Gibeah (20:37). Rather, they attempt to annihilate the whole tribe of Benjamin—not just its military forces, but also "the city, the people, the animals, and all that remained" (20:48). In short, what the united Israelites had *failed* to do in Judges 1—that is, devoting the Canaanites to destruction, according to God's command and in keeping with the theology of "holy war" (see the exception in 1:17, as well as the "holy war" provisions in Deuteronomy 20)—they *succeed* in doing in Judges 20, but *against their own people!* Everything is wrong!

Of course, the Benjaminites themselves did not help their cause much. They refused to turn over the guilty men of Gibeah to the assembled Israelites, and they were all too ready to fight to defend this stupid and selfish decision (see 20:12–17). But again, this underscores the narrator's point that *everything and everybody were wrong;* because the people—Israelites, Benjaminites, Levites—were doing "what was right in their own eyes." When this situation persisted, the only possible result was violence and more violence.

Given the Torah stipulations that allow for retribution, perhaps it is too much to expect that the gathered Israelites might have been gracious toward the Benjaminites, at least toward the Benjaminites not directly implicated in the crime. On the other hand, the Torah story is one that relates over and over again how God forgave a guilty people (see Introduction, section 4). Furthermore, the structure of the book of Judges hinges on the kind of God who constantly forgives the sinful people, thus allowing their story to continue. Indeed, a crucial piece of the repeated pattern in the book of Judges is God's deliverance of the people; because God "would be moved to pity by their groaning because of those who persecuted and oppressed them" (2:18). The Hebrew root translated "moved to pity" is *nhm,* which recurs twice in chapter 21 to describe the reaction of the Israelites to Benjamin's plight (see NRSV, "had compassion" in vv. 6, 15).

Hence, perhaps it is not too much to expect that the Israelites would have shown compassion to the Benjaminites from the beginning, treating them graciously as God had repeatedly treated Israel graciously in the Torah narrative (see *nhm* in Exod. 32:12, 14; NRSV "change your mind" and "changed his mind") and throughout the book of Judges, as anticipated by 2:18. In fact, although it is pitifully late, the Israelites seem poised in 21:6 to embody the kind of gracious compassion that they had repeatedly received from God. Their belated compassion for Benjamin is on the right track, and "peace" (21:13) is properly their goal; but the Israelites blow it again.

The ridiculous question the people address to God in 21:3 is perhaps evidence enough that the Israelites have really not made much progress. They should have known full well why one tribe is lacking, because they themselves were responsible for wiping out Benjamin! In any case, in attempting to address this lack and to apply their newly found compassion to the six hundred surviving Benjaminites (see 20:47), the people simply fall again into violent folly. Their so-called compassion toward Benjamin is effected by further violence as they proceed to wipe out the population of Jabesh-gilead (21:8–12; compare again 1 Sam. 11—that is, the people now do what later Saul will prevent the Ammonites from doing), except for the four hundred virgins who are reserved for the surviving men of Benjamin. That they justify their attempt at compassion with reference to solemn oaths (see 21:1, 5) is not much of a defense, given the poor history of oaths in the book of Judges (see 11:29–40). Besides, the framework of Judges 17—21 (see 17:6; 21:25) makes suspect any claim on the part of the people that they are doing anything in relation to God or God's will. From every appearance, any oath they had sworn would have amounted to nothing more than using God's name wrongly (see Exod. 20:7). In any case, the so-called peace extended to Benjamin is effected at a horrible cost.

As if their first attempt is not bad enough, the Israelites try again, since two hundred more surviving Benjaminites need wives. The note of pity and compassion is repeated in v. 15, and the reader hears again about the need for wives (vv. 16–17) and the solemn oath (v. 18). The strategy this second time is a bit less violent, but hardly satisfactory. In essence, the Israelites sanction the stealing of the young women of Shiloh (vv. 19–24). As Trible puts it, summarizing the effect of the Israelites' two attempts at compassion, "the rape of one has become the rape of six hundred" (Trible, p. 83). Things simply could not have gotten any worse. Olson's summary is helpful as well, although perhaps understated:

> When the Israelite tribes totally annihilated Jabesh-Gilead and sanctioned the kidnapping of the women of Shiloh in order to protect themselves from breaking their vow, they give evidence of having lost their moral and covenantal bearings. Preoccupation with legalistic and technical obedience to certain rules or laws without an accompanying sense of the principles of faithfulness and love that undergird such laws and temper their rigid application is a recipe for disaster. (Olson, 887)

136

That the people have "lost their moral and covenantal bearings" is precisely what the narrator means when he closes the book of Judges with the observation that frames chapters 17—21: "In those days there was no king in Israel; all the people did what was right in their own eyes" (21:25; see 17:6).

In a real sense, of course, the people in the book of Judges never really had "their moral and covenantal bearings." From the beginning, they failed to honor God's sole sovereignty and to maintain covenant loyalty. Instead, they were self-assertive and idolatrous (see the commentary on 1:1—2:5); and the plot of the book of Judges revolves around God's gracious and repeated attempts to call the people back to faithfulness and obedience. But, after the early successes of Othniel, Ehud, Deborah/Barak/Jael, there is a marked turn for the worse with Gideon; and things deteriorate progressively before hitting bottom in Judges 17—21.

So the book of Judges is finally a book of weeping (see 2:1–5; 11:37–38; 20:23, 26; 21:2). The tragedy of errors in chapters 17—21 suggests that things simply cannot get any worse. As if yielding to the unspeakable horror, the narrator repeats the observation of 17:16; and the book of Judges reaches its ignominious end.

Reflections: Chaos and Crisis, Then and Now

As has been previously suggested several times, it is easy for contemporary readers of the book of Judges to dismiss it as a collection of barbaric stories from a primitive and relatively uncivilized time. To do this, however, is both a disservice to the book of Judges and to ourselves. The book of Judges focuses our attention on an issue of perennial importance for the human community—that is, how to achieve justice and peace among human beings who seem inevitably to be self-centered and self-assertive. If, as argued above on the basis of chapters 17—21 and the entire book of Judges, idolatry and self-assertion ultimately and inevitably produce violence, then the book of Judges could hardly be more timely.

It is tempting to forget that the world has recently witnessed the passing of a century that proved to be the most violent century in the history of humankind, although the ominous beginning of the twenty-first century—particularly September 11, 2001, and its aftermath—may force us to remember. Even so, contemporary North Americans seem inclined to accept almost no responsibility for the desperate and deplorable conditions that breed terrorism in certain parts of the world. So, at the beginning of the twenty-first century, it is apparently still easy for citizens of the United States to pretend that we are not complicit in

137

the violence of the world. Not coincidentally in relation to all of this, writer Walker Percy dubbed the twentieth century "The Century of the Self." The "autonomous self," according to Percy, is the most dangerous entity imaginable (12, 156).

Knowing no limits other than what is right in its own eyes, the autonomous self can and does fall prey to almost any ideology. As for citizens of the United States, we live in a society that systematically teaches us to be autonomous—that is, literally understood, to be laws unto ourselves (*autos,* self, and *nomos,* law). This was precisely the problem in Judges 17—21—"all the people did what was right in their own eyes." Again, the book of Judges, especially perhaps chapters 17—21, could hardly be more timely.

Psychologists, sociologists, anthropologists, philosophers, theologians, and politicians frequently contemplate the reasons for the chaos and deep-seated crisis in contemporary North American society, especially the loss of social connectedness and the epidemic violence. But the cause of the crisis is not really so mysterious. The book of Judges, from beginning to end, but especially in chapters 17—21, demonstrates in a compelling manner that idolatry—for instance, in the form of the elevation of the self to the status of a god—will inevitably result in chaos and violence.

Granted, the violence in the book of Judges, especially chapters 17—21, is shocking, but hardly as shocking as the evening news on any given night. Indeed, the book of Judges needs to be shocking in order to reach people, then and now, who are thoroughly self-absorbed. Writer Flannery O'Connor, who was often criticized for writing stories that are grotesque and gruesome, was actually a profound interpreter of, and advocate for, the centrality of grace. Her stories are shocking, she once said, because contemporary persons are so self-absorbed that they *have to be* shocked into hearing the message of grace.

Something similar can be said for the book of Judges, especially chapters 17—21. By graphically portraying the shocking consequences of idolatry and self-assertion, chapters 17—21 open the way for hearing the message that lies within and around the book of Judges. The book of Judges, and the larger canonical story of which it is a part, portray a God who would not—indeed, *could* not—stop loving a persistently idolatrous and frustratingly faithless people. So, in the book of Judges, the people are forgiven and delivered again and again and again, until things finally fall completely apart. But the book of Judges is not the end of the story. God will try again to establish in and through human beings and human structures the justice, righteousness, and

138

peace that God wills; and God is trying still. So the book of Judges, especially when heard within its larger canonical context, is ultimately a call
to covenant loyalty as it witnesses to the amazing reality that "explains"
God's incredible perseverance—an unfailing love that is inevitably
manifest as grace.

BIBLIOGRAPHY

Commentaries and Resources for Teaching and Preaching

Amit, Yairah. *Judges: Introduction and Commentary.* Mikra le-Yisra'el, A Bible Commentary for Israel. Tel Aviv: Am Oved/Jerusalem: Magnes/The Hebrew University Press, 1999.

Boling, Robert G. *Judges.* Anchor Bible 6A. New York: Doubleday, 1975.

Brenner, Athalya, ed. *A Feminist Companion to Judges.* Feminist Companion to the Bible 4. Sheffield: Sheffield Academic Press, 1993.

Farmer, Kathleen A. *Joshua, Judges, Ruth.* Journey through the Bible, vol. 3. Nashville: Cokesbury, 1994.

Fewell, Danna Nolan. "Judges." In *The Women's Bible Commentary,* edited by Carol A. Newsom and Sharon H. Ringe, 67–77. Louisville, Ky.: Westminster John Knox, 1992.

Fretheim, Terence E. *Deuteronomic History.* Interpreting Biblical Texts. Nashville: Abingdon, 1983.

Gray, John. *Joshua, Judges, Ruth.* New Century Bible Commentary. Grand Rapids: Eerdmans, 1986.

Hamlin, E. John. *Judges: At Risk in the Promised Land.* International Theological Commentary. Grand Rapids: Eerdmans, 1990.

Jeter, Joseph R., Jr. *Preaching Judges.* St. Louis: Chalice, 2002.

Mayes, J. D. H. *Judges.* Sheffield: JSOT Press, 1985.

Moore, George. *Judges.* International Critical Commentary. New York: Harper, 1969.

Nelson, Richard D. *The Historical Books.* Interpreting Biblical Texts. Nashville: Abingdon, 1998.

Olson, Dennis T. "Introduction, Commentary, and Reflections on the Book of Judges." In *The New Interpreter's Bible,* vol. 2, 723–888. Nashville: Abingdon, 1998.

Schneiders, Tammy J. *Judges.* Berit Olam: Studies in Hebrew Narrative and Poetry. Collegeville, Minn.: Liturgical Press, 2000.

Soggin, J. Alberto. *Judges, A Commentary.* Old Testament Library. Translated by J. S. Bowden. Philadelphia: Westminster, 1981.

Tate, Marvin E. *From Promise to Exile: The Former Prophets.* Macon, Ga.: Smyth & Helwys, 1998.

Trible, Phyllis. *Texts of Terror: Literary-Feminist Readings of Biblical Narratives.* Overtures to Biblical Theology. Philadelphia: Fortress, 1984.

Wilcock, Michael. *The Message of Judges: Grace Abounding.* The Bible Speaks Today. Downers Grove, Ill.: InterVarsity, 1992.

Yee, Gale A., ed., *Judges and Method: New Approaches in Biblical Studies.* Minneapolis: Fortress, 1995.

Literature Cited

Ackerman, Susan. *Warrior, Dancer, Seductress, Queen: Women in Judges and Biblical Israel.* New York: Doubleday, 1998.

Alter, Robert. "Samson without Folklore." In *Text and Tradition,* edited by Susan Niditch, 47–73. Atlanta: Scholars Press, 1990.

Amit, Yairah."Judges 4: Its Contents and Form," *Journal for the Study of the Old Testament* 39:89–111 (1987).

———. "Hidden Polemic in the Conquest of Dan: Judges XVII-XVIII," *Vetus Testamentum* 40:4–20 (1990).

Auld, A. Graeme. "Gideon: Hacking at the Heart of the Old Testament," *Vetus Testamentum* 39:257–67 (1989).

Bal, Mieke. *Death and Dissymmetry: The Politics of Coherence in the Book of Judges.* Chicago Studies in the History of Judaism. Chicago: University of Chicago Press, 1988.

Berquist, Jon L. *Reclaiming Her Story: The Witness of Women in the Old Testament.* St. Louis: Chalice, 1992.

Bledstein, Adrian Janis. "Is Judges a Woman's Satire of Men Who Play God?" In *A Feminist Companion to Judges,* edited by Athalya Brenner, 34–54. Sheffield: JSOT Press, 1993.

Boling, Robert G. *Judges.* Anchor Bible 6A. New York: Doubleday, 1975.

Bowman, Richard G. "Narrative Criticism: Human Purpose in Conflict with Divine Presence." In *Judges and Method: New Approaches in Biblical Studies,* edited by Gale A. Yee, 17–44. Minneapolis: Fortress, 1995.

Brenner, Athalya, ed. *A Feminist Companion to Judges.* The Feminist Companion to the Bible 4. Sheffield: JSOT Press, 1993.

Cousar, Charles B. *A Theology of the Cross: The Death of Jesus in the Pauline Letters.* Overtures to Biblical Theology. Minneapolis: Fortress, 1990.

Crenshaw, James. *Samson: A Secret Betrayed, a Vow Ignored.* Atlanta: John Knox, 1978.

Crump, Galbraith M., ed. *Twentieth Century Interpretations of Samson Agonistes: A Collection of Critical Essays.* Englewood Cliffs, N.J.: Prentice-Hall, 1968.

Elizondo, Virgilio. *Galilean Journey: The Mexican-American Promise.* Maryknoll, N.Y.: Orbis, 1983.

Exum, J. Cheryl. "Murder They Wrote: Ideology and Manipulation of Female Presence in Biblical Narrative," *Union Seminary Quarterly Review* 43:19–39 (1989).

―――. *Tragedy and Biblical Narrative: Arrows of the Almighty.* Cambridge: Cambridge University Press, 1992.

Fewell, Danna Nolan. "Judges." In *The Women's Bible Commentary,* edited by Carol A. Newsom and Sharon H. Ringe, 67–77. Louisville, Ky.: Westminster John Knox, 1992.

―――. "Deconstructive Criticism: Achsah and the [E]razed City of Writing." In *Judges and Method: New Approaches in Biblical Studies,* edited by Gale A. Yee, 119–45. Minneapolis: Fortress, 1995.

Fretheim, Terence. *The Suffering of God: An Old Testament Perspective.* Overtures to Biblical Theology. Philadelphia: Fortress, 1984.

―――. *Exodus.* Interpretation: A Bible Commentary for Teaching and Preaching. Atlanta: John Knox, 1991.

Fuchs, Esther. "Marginalization, Ambiguity, Silencing: The Story of Jephthah's Daughter," *Journal of Feminist Studies in Religion* 5:35–45 (1989).

Grieb, A. Katherine. "Feminist or Faithful: How Scripture Teaches a Hermeneutic of Suspicion." Paper delivered at the 1997 Annual Meeting of the Society of Biblical Literature, November 22, 1997, San Francisco, California. Later published in slightly different form in *Suwanee Theological Review* 41:261–76 (Pentecost 1998).

Hall, Douglas John. *Christian Mission: The Stewardship of Life in the Kingdom of Death.* New York: Friendship Press, 1985.

―――. *God and Human Suffering: An Exercise in the Theology of the Cross.* Minneapolis: Augsburg, 1986.

Hamlin, E. John. *Judges: At Risk in the Promised Land.* International Theolgical Commentary. Grand Rapids: Eerdmans, 1990.

Hauerwas, Stanley, and William Willimon. *Resident Aliens: Life in the Christian Colony.* Nashville: Abingdon, 1989.

―――. *Where Resident Aliens Live: Exercises for Christian Practice.* Nashville: Abingdon, 1996.

Howard, David M., Jr. *An Introduction to the Old Testament Historical Books.* Chicago: Moody, 1993.

Howell, James C. "The Primrose Path of Dalliance." A sermon delivered on "The Protestant Hour," May 19, 1996 *(www.prtvc.org/ sermons/ph96/ph-96–20.htm).*

Hudson, Don Michael. "Living in a Land of Epithets: Anonymity in Judges 19–21," *Journal for the Study of the Old Testament* 62:49–66 (1994).

Jeter, Joseph R., Jr. *Preaching Judges.* St. Louis: Chalice, 2002.

Jones-Warsaw, Koala. "Toward a Womanist Hermeneutic: A Reading of Judges 19–21," *Journal of the Interdenominational Theological Center* 22:18–35 (1994).

Keefe, Alice A. "Rapes of Women/Wars of Men." In *Women, War, and Metaphor: Language and Society in the Study of the Hebrew Bible,* edited by Claudia V. Camp and Carole R. Fontaine. *Semeia* 61:79–97 (1993).

Klein, Lillian R. *The Triumph of Irony in the Book of Judges.* JSOTSup 68. Sheffield: Almond Press, 1988.

Koch, Klaus. *The Prophets: The Assyrian Period.* Translated by Margaret Kohl. Philadelphia: Fortress, 1982.

Lasine, Stuart. "Guest and Host in Judges 19: Lot's Hospitality in an Inverted World," *Journal for the Study of the Old Testament* 29:37–59 (1984).

Matthews, Victor H. "Freedom and Entrapment in the Samson Narrative: A Literary Analysis," *Perspectives in Religious Studies* 16:245–57 (1989).

———. "Hospitality and Hostility in Judges 4," *Biblical Theology Bulletin* 21:13–21 (1991).

———. "Hospitality and Hostility in Genesis 19 and Judges 19," *Biblical Theology Bulletin* 22:3–11 (1992).

———. "Female Voices Upholding the Honor of the Household," *Biblical Theology Bulletin* 24:8–15 (1994).

———. *Old Testament Themes.* St. Louis: Chalice, 2000.

Nelson, Richard. *First and Second Kings.* Interpretation: A Bible Commentary for Teaching and Preaching. Atlanta: John Knox, 1987.

Niditch, Susan. "Eroticism and Death in the Tale of Jael." In *Gender and Difference in Ancient Israel,* edited by Peggy L. Day, 43–57. Minneapolis: Fortress, 1989.

———. "Samson as Culture Hero, Trickster, and Bandit: The Empowerment of the Weak," *Catholic Biblical Quarterly* 52:608–24 (1990).

Niebuhr, H. Richard. *Christ and Culture.* New York: Harper and Row, 1951.

Olson, Dennis T. "Introduction, Commentary, and Reflections on the Book of Judges." In *The New Interpreter's Bible,* vol. 2, 723–888. Nashville: Abingdon, 1998.

Percy, Walker. *Lost in the Cosmos: The Last Self-Help Book.* New York: Washington Square Press, 1983.

Placher, William C. *Narratives of a Vulnerable God: Christ, Theology and Scripture.* Louisville, Ky.: Westminster John Knox, 1994.

Reinhartz, Adele. "Samson's Mother: An Unnamed Protagonist," *Journal for the Study of the Old Testament* 55:25–37 (1992).

Römer, Thomas C. "Why Would the Deuteronomists Tell about the Sacrifice of Jephthah's Daughter?" *Journal for the Study of the Old Testament* 77:27–38 (1998).

Sanders, James. *Torah and Canon.* Philadelphia: Fortress, 1972.

Satterthwaite, Philip. "'No King in Israel': Narrative Criticism and Judges 17–21," *Tyndale Bulletin* 44:76–88 (1993).

Schneiders, Tammi J. *Judges.* Berit Olam: Studies in Hebrew Narrative and Poetry. Collegeville, Minn.: Liturgical Press, 2000.

Soggin, J. Alberto. *Judges: A Commentary.* Old Testament Library. Translated by J. S. Bowden. Philadelphia: Westminster, 1981.

Tanner, J. Paul. "The Gideon Narrative as the Focal Point of Judges," *Bibliotheca Sacra* 149:146–61 (1992).

Tate, Marvin E. *From Promise to Exile: The Former Prophets.* Macon, Ga.: Smyth & Helwys, 1998.

Trible, Phyllis. *Texts of Terror: Literary-Feminist Readings of Biblical Narratives.* Overtures to Biblical Theology. Philadelphia: Fortress, 1984.

Tutu, Desmond. *No Future without Forgiveness.* New York: Doubleday/Image, 1999.

Walsh, J. P. M. *The Mighty from Their Thrones: Power in the Biblical Tradition.* Overtures to Biblical Theology. Philadelphia: Fortress, 1987.

Warrior, Robert Allen. "Canaanites, Cowboys, and Indians: Deliverance, Conquest, and Liberation Theology Today," *Christianity and Crisis,* September 11, 1989, 261–65.

Webb, Barry G. *The Book of Judges: An Integrated Reading.* JSOTSup 46. Sheffield: JSOT Press, 1987.

Wessels, J. P. M. "'Postmodern' Rhetoric and the Former Prophetic Literature." In *Rhetoric, Scripture, and Theology: Essays from the 1994 Pretoria Conference,* edited by S. E. Porter and T. H. Olbricht, 182–94. JSNTSup 131. Sheffield: Sheffield Academic Press, 1996.

Wharton, James A. "The Secret of Yahweh: Story and Affirmation in Judges 13–16," *Interpretation* 27:48–66 (1973).

Wilcock, Michael. *The Message of Judges: Grace Abounding.* The Bible Speaks Today. Downers Grove, Ill.: InterVarsity, 1992.

Yee, Gale A., ed. *Judges and Method: New Approaches in Biblical Studies.* Minneapolis: Fortress, 1995.

145

Younger, K. Lawson. "Judges 1 in Its Near Eastern Literary Context." In *Faith, Tradition, and History,* edited by A. R. Millard, J. K. Hoffmeier, and D. W. Baker, 207–27. Winona Lake, Ind.: Eisenbrauns, 1994.